U.S. Airborne
in action

By Leroy Thompson

Color by Ken MacSwan

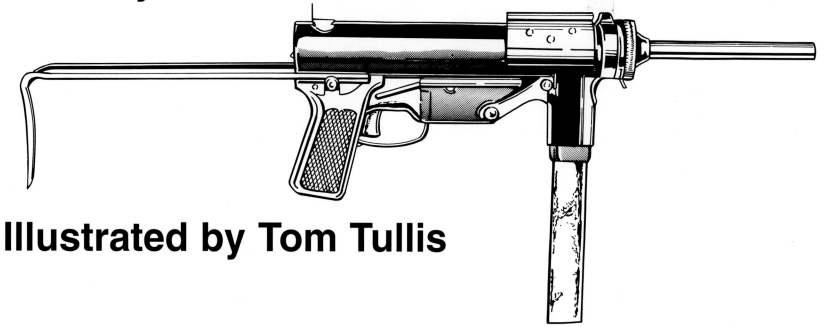

Illustrated by Tom Tullis

Combat Troops Number 10
squadron/signal publications

A member of the 101st Airborne Division attacks the crew of a German Hetzer self-propelled gun during the drive into Germany. The paratrooper is armed with an M1A1 Carbine and grenades.

ISBN 0-89747-283-7

If you have any photographs of aircraft, armor, soldiers or ships of any nation, particularly wartime snapshots, why not share them with us and help make Squadron/Signal's books all the more interesting and complete in the future. Any photograph sent to us will be copied and the original returned. The donor will be fully credited for any photos used. Please send them to:

Squadron/Signal Publications, Inc.
1115 Crowley Drive
Carrollton, TX 75011-5010

Acknowledgements

U.S. Army

Bundesarchiv

Imperial War Museum (IWM)

U.S. Air Force (USAF)

Dedication:

To all the men who jumped out of perfectly good aircraft during WW II, Korea, Vietnam, Grenada, and Persian Gulf War.

U.S. Army Parachute Badge

U.S. Army Glider Badge

A paratrooper of the 82nd Airborne demonstrates proper technique for standing in the door of a C-47 prior to jumping. The trooper is armed with an M1 Garand .30 caliber rifle. (U.S. Army)

3

U.S. Airborne

Although the fertile mind of Billy Mitchell had toyed with the formation of an airborne trained force to be created from the 1st Infantry Division during the First World War, it was not until more than two decades later that the idea of parachute infantry was really taken seriously in the upper echelons of the U.S. War Department. Since the Soviet Union and Germany had proceeded with the development of parachute forces, the Assistant Chief of Staff sent a memorandum to the Chief of Infantry on 1 May 1939 requesting a study of the feasibility of "air infantry." This study, when completed, suggested that air infantry could be tasked with hazardous missions behind enemy lines, reconnaissance, seizure and holding of key objectives and drops ahead of advancing mechanized forces – many of the missions which would eventually define the capabilities of parachute, airmobile and special forces.

Initially, consideration was given to the formation of "Air Grenadiers" which would be part of the Army Air Corps, but the lack of transport aircraft led this idea to be shelved. As the idea of airborne forces spread after World War II, some countries did see the logic of parachute infantry within their air forces. In January of 1940, the air infantry project again received high priority after the Soviet invasion of Finland. During this action, the Soviets had dropped airborne forces, at least some reportedly without parachutes into deep snow banks! MGEN George Lynch, the Chief of Infantry, assigned one of his most able subordinates, MAJ Bill Lee to the air infantry project and in late February of 1940, Fort Benning's Infantry Board submitted a recommendation that a proper parachute be developed and a 40-man platoon be formed to test the parachute infantry concept.

The result of this recommendation was the approval of the T-4 parachute with a twenty-eight foot main canopy and a reserve parachute with a twenty-two foot canopy. The development of this parachute resulted in the go-ahead being received for the formation of the "Test Platoon."

Volunteers were taken from the 29th Infantry Regiment at Fort Benning. Everyone was surprised by the enthusiasm for the idea and there were over 200 enlisted volunteers on the first day as well as seventeen officer volunteers. Two names, which would later become famous in U.S. airborne history, were among those first officers – William T. Ryder and William P. Yarborough. In light of the enthusiasm, the Infantry Board decided to select 48 enlisted men broken into four 12-man squads, the eight extra men being included because of the large number of anticipated training injuries. LT Ryder, who had previously written articles on the need for an airborne force, passed the written test given the officer candidates with flying colors and was selected to command the platoon. Unfortunately, his friend Yarborough had been transferred to another command before having a chance to take the test.

To give the actual training, a number of Air Corps Parachute Jumping Instructors (PJIs) were assigned to the unit. The Infantry Board also devised a tough eight-week physical training schedule, which included hand-to-hand combat, calisthenics, tumbling, daily three-mile runs and Parachute Landing Falls (PLFs). Although already in great shape since they had been tactical demonstration troops for the Infantry School, the volunteers still found the regime rigorous. Nevertheless, the highly motivated troops soon asked to raise the daily runs to five miles. The tradition of "pushing down Georgia," known to many future generations of paratroops, also began with ten pushups being assigned for even minor infractions. Today, that ten is really eleven as everyone adds: "one more for airborne."

It soon became apparent that another officer was desirable in the test platoon so 2LT James A. Basset was assigned after training had already begun. MAJ Lee himself made periodic trips to observe training and retained an interest even when at his desk. Lee, for example, learned of two 150-foot parachute towers in Hightstown, New Jersey and arranged for the platoon to fly to Fort Dix for ten days of training on the towers. During this period the Chief of Infantry, MGEN Lynch, visited and tried a jump, winning the respect of the Test Platoon and getting a first hand feel for their training.

Upon their return to Fort Benning, members of the Test Platoon learned to pack their own parachutes and anticipated their eighth week of training when they would make five jumps from an aircraft. The first jumps were successful though one of the paratroops who had made it all the way through training found he could not "exit a plane in flight"

This 250-foot tower at Fort Benning was used to train parachute troops. This tower was based on one at Hightstown, New Jersey, which was used in training the original members of the test platoon. (U.S. Army)

and was dropped from the platoon. The final jump was a mass jump by the entire platoon from three aircraft under the watchful eyes of the brass from the Infantry Board as well as GEN George Marshall and the Secretary of War Henry Stimson. Their training complete, members of the Test Platoon were broken into two groups; one under LT Basset to go to Chanute Field to learn parachute rigging, the other under LT Ryder to stay to form the nucleus of a parachute training unit.

Spurred by the successes of the German *Fallschirmjägers* in Europe, the Infantry Board pushed for the formation of the first full parachute battalion – the 501st – and volunteers began pouring in to Fort Benning for training. The concept now having been proven, there were some attempts by the Army Engineers and Army Air Corps to gain control of the parachute troops, but the decision was made that no matter how they were delivered, the paratroops were still parachute infantrymen and they stayed under the Infantry Branch.

MAJ William Miley, Fort Benning's athletic officer, was named to command the new 501st Parachute Battalion, while volunteers for the battalion were accepted from commands all over the U.S. By November of 1940, the men were assembled and ready for training. To assist in preparing Miley's training areas, MAJ Lee helped get drop zones cleared at Fort Benning and arranged for two 250-foot parachute towers to be built. Later, thirty-four foot towers and aircraft mockups were added. Even before the 501st Battalion was trained, the War Department, under the impending threat of war, ordered three more parachute battalions to be formed.

By January of 1941, most members of the 501st Battalion were parachute qualified and Miley authorized qualified paratroopers to wear their jump boots with trousers bloused, a "501" over their Infantry Branch insignia and an "overseas" cap with the parachute cap badge. Additionally, the Department of Heraldry informed Miley that a distinctive parachute qualification badge was to be authorized and sent along a possible design. One of Miley's staff officers, LT William Yarborough, created the design, which was eventually adopted. The creative Yarborough also suggested the distinctive parachute oval backing to show unit affiliation and designed the parachutist's uniform (with pockets accessible even when wearing a parachute harness) and the famous jump boots.

On 10 March 1941, the Provisional Parachute Group was formed at Fort Benning using members of the 501st Parachute Battalion as the cadre to train future paratroopers. Recently promoted LTC Lee commanded the group with the mission of developing air-borne Table of Organization and Equipment (TO&E) as well as carrying out parachute training. On 28 June 1941, the 501st Parachute Infantry Battalion (PIB) deployed to Panama to carry out exercises with the 550th Air Landing Battalion, a unit designed to be air transported to battle, possibly to an airfield seized by the 501st. These two units were also present in Panama as a counter to a perceived German threat to the Panama Canal. While stationed there, airborne officers made contingency plans for carrying out jumps over various Lain American capitals should their capture prove necessary!

A few months later, in July of 1941, the 502nd PIB was activated at Fort Benning, while in the same month the Air Corps began experimenting with gliders. As the threat of war in the Pacific and Europe increased, the rapid expansion of the new airborne forces continued with the activation of the 503rd PIB in August. The Fall 1941 maneuvers in Panama had proven so successful that another Air Landing Battalion, the 88th, was activated at Fort Benning in October. Command and control over the burgeoning parachute and air landing forces was proving difficult as the original War Department

Members of the Parachute Test Platoon float down to the Drop Zone (DZ) during an early practice jump. Practice jumps began during the eighth week of training. (U.S. Army)

CAPT J.W. Coutts inspects the parachutes of these troopers of the Parachute Test Platoon prior to a jump. He has a parachutist's cap insignia on his garrison cap. The troopers are wearing the early style jumpsuits and cloth helmets. (U.S. Army)

concept had not anticipated that airborne troops would be used in formations larger than battalions; therefore, no headquarters larger than a battalion HQ existed in the organizational structure.

In January of 1942, on the heels of the Pearl Harbor attack, the War Department ordered the formation of four parachute regiments using the existing battalions as the basis. To give more cohesion and control of these units, in March of 1942, the Airborne Command was formed under Lee, who was promoted to full Colonel. The command was established at Fort Benning and was directly under Army Ground Force HQ. To facilitate the availability of aircrews trained to work with parachute troops, the Air Corps established Air Transport Command (ATC), later to become Troop Carrier Command.

Originally, ATC had C-47s, which had only one exit door, although these were augmented later by C-46s, which had two doors. Despite the C-46's outstanding features for paratroop usage, virtually all combat jumps during the war were from C-47s.

For glider troops, the 3,750-pound Waco CG-4A was the original glider chosen for development. Glider training centers were eventually established at Sedalia, MO; Alliance, NE, and Laurinburg-Maxton Army Air Base, NC with the latter being the primary facility in the program. The first actual glider unit was the former 88th Air Landing Battalion, which became the 88th Glider Infantry Regiment (GIR). While waiting to receive their gliders, this unit put their previous training to good use as they trained conventional infantry troops in air landing and air movement. Despite the various hazards associated with glider landings, it would not be until July of 1944 that glider troops would achieve pay parity with parachute troops.

The first unit actually deployed to the war in Europe was the 2nd Battalion/503rd Parachute Infantry Regiment (PIR) under LTC Edson Raff, which sailed for the United Kingdom on 6 June 1942.

After landing, troopers of the Test Platoon retrieve their weapons from an equipment roll that was dropped with them. They are armed with M1917 revolvers and M1 Garand rifles. (U.S. Army)

LT Ryder, Commander of the Parachute Test Battalion (walking from right), and other members of the platoon prepare to board a Douglas C-47 Skytrain transport for a training jump. (U.S. Army)

The first free descent made by members of the Parachute Test Platoon, and virtually every other American paratrooper trained since then, was from one of these towers at Fort Benning, GA. (U.S. Army)

That same summer, a Parachute Test Battery was formed to test the concept of airborne artillery and methods for its deployment. For initial use, the battery chose the Pack 75MM Howitzer originally designed for mule transport by mountain artillery units. The basic unit, which evolved, was a 108-man battery equipped with four Pack Howitzers, the entire battery being capable of being dropped by nine C-47s. This Test Battery soon became the basis for the 456th Parachute Field Artillery Battalion activated on 24 September 1942. This would be the first of twelve Parachute Field Artillery Battalions to be activated during the war. The need for a more powerful, longer ranging artillery piece was apparent from the beginning and in 1943 the Army developed a 105MM Howitzer especially adapted to fit into a CG-4A glider. Nine of the more heavily equipped glider field artillery battalions would be formed during the war.

20 July 1942 also saw the formation of still more parachute infantry regiments with the 506th and 507th being activated. Lee was also promoted to Brigadier General and sent to visit the British airborne forces where he learned they were planning to form airborne divisions. Upon his return he recommended that the Army do the same.

At Ground Force HQ, GEN McNair studied Lee's recommendation and then gave the go-ahead to form two airborne divisions – the 82nd and 101st. The new divisions would have an authorized strength of 8,321 troops, about half the size of a normal infantry division. Initially, it was planned that each division would be comprised of one parachute infantry regiment and two glider infantry regiments. This TO&E was soon switched to include two parachute infantry regiments and one glider infantry regiment as well as airborne signals, engineers and artillery and other support troops. Original commanders of the divisions were Matthew Ridgway for the 82nd and William Lee for the 101st. These new divisions were officially activated on 15 August 1942.

A parachute trainee is hoisted into position for a free descent from one of the 250-foot training towers at Fort Benning. Jumps from these towers helped condition the trainees and gave them practice in landings under more controlled conditions than an actual jump from an aircraft. (U.S. Army)

These two early parachute trainees are about to be released from the 250-foot training tower. The empty parachute holder on the right is being lowered to load another trainee. (U.S. Army)

Operation TORCH and the North African Campaign

The first major European U.S. Combat involvement, although selected American personnel had gone on operations with British Special Forces, was Operation TORCH, scheduled for 8 November 1942. Since the landings would be against French colonies where feelings ran high against the British (as a result of the Royal Navy attack on the French fleet at Oran during 1940) it was decided that the landings should appear to be an American operation. The British, however, would launch a simultaneous attack against the *Afrika Korps* out of Egypt, catching GEN Rommel in a pincer movement.

The airborne phase of TORCH was suggested by MGEN Mark Clark, Eisenhower's deputy and a strong supporter of airborne forces. Clark's airborne staff officer was the same MAJ William Yarborough who had helped design the airborne insignia and uniform. The mission, which was assigned to the American airborne forces, was the seizure, by the 509th Parachute Infantry, of two key airfields just south of Oran on D Day. This mission would require the paratroopers to fly 1,500 miles from airfields in the UK, then jump and seize the airfields. Since it was unsure whether they would meet French resistance, Yarborough was ordered to prepare two plans – one based on a combat jump, the other on a peaceful air landing.

The resultant plan for LTC Edson D. Raff's battalion called for an air landing at La Senia Airfield or a combat jump on Tafaraoui Airfield. Should the combat jump be called for, the paratroopers would also have the mission of destroying French fighter aircraft at both airfields. Theoretically, the aircraft were to be guided in by a radar beacon emplaced by a U.S. agent. Although the troopers were not told their objective, they were supplied with intelligence photos from the British, models of the airfields were constructed and the missions were rehearsed again and again.

On 7 November with the paratroopers on five-minute standby, they received a coded communication that the French would cooperate. That night, 556 paratroopers packed into thirty-nine C-47s took off for the long flight to North Africa. During the flight, the formation became scattered as the paratroopers tried to get a few hours of fitful sleep. Meanwhile, in French North Africa, French troops were put on alert after spotting the approaching armada of ships. It looked as if they might choose to fight after all! Although a plan was in effect to alert the transports should the situation change, the radio operator aboard the ship assigned this mission was on a different radio frequency from the transport aircraft and they did not learn that they might have to make a combat jump.

For some aircraft it was a moot point, since they had strayed so far off course that they ended up in Spanish Morocco. Twenty-one aircraft, which had managed to reach La Senia, tried to land and were met with a hail of anti-aircraft fire. Most managed to divert and land on a dry salt lakebed west of Oran. Eventually, more aircraft landed along with Raff and Yarborough, though Raff had been injured when he jumped with a few sticks of paratroopers near the lakebed due to a misunderstanding. Attempting to complete their mission, Yarborough led one company of paratroopers in three of the aircraft on a short hop to Tafaraoui Airfield, but French fighters attacked the aircraft, killing seven paratroopers and wounding twenty. After the aircraft crash-landed, the paratroopers continued to advance on the airfield, which had already been secured by advancing U.S. ground troops.

Although initially the French had resisted, as Raff's paratroopers discovered to their loss, the German occupation of Vichy France soon engendered French cooperation in North Africa. There were still, however, the remnants of the reinforced *Afrika Korps* to be dealt with. As a result, the 509th was alerted on 10 November to be prepared for a mission in support of the British 1st Army's advance on Tunis. Raff was called to Algiers where he learned his battalion's mission was to jump on 15 November to secure another French airfield at Tebessa near the Tunisian border. To make the mission more "interesting", Raff learned that there was a strong possibility that German paratroopers might occupy the airfield ahead of him. Raff's plan called for two companies plus a number of additional specialized troops to jump directly onto the airfield.

On the day before the mission, however, the objective changed when Raff learned of another larger airfield at Yaks les Bains. It was decided to jump at this site, and then send one company to march on Tebessa to capture it as well. 350 paratroopers aboard twenty-two C-47s beat the Germans to the objective and seized it unopposed. Company D dug in around the airfield, while Company E was sent to occupy Tebessa, where they dug in as well. Later reinforced by other troops, the paratroopers held these airfields for more than a week. Not content with a static defensive role, however, the paratroopers carried out aggressive patrols across the border into Tunisia, where on one operation they took 200 prisoners. As the Germans stopped the Allied advance and even pushed it back, the members of the 509th were used as elite infantry to fill in at critical points, often in company strength.

Another mission soon arose which was far more suited to the role of parachute infantry. Although cutting Rommel's supply lines had been given top priority, the railway bridge at El Djem could not be knocked out by air strikes. As a result, it was

Troopers of the 82nd Airborne inspect equipment containers prior to a practice jump in North Africa during June of 1943. The trooper in the foreground has a rope coil attached to his harness, an item paratroopers often found invaluable. The trooper at the right in the background graphically illustrates why the enemy called American paratroops, "devils in baggy pants." (U.S. Army)

decided to send an airborne raiding party to destroy it. To carry out the mission, 2LT Dan De Leon and thirty-two paratroopers would jump ninety miles behind the German lines on Christmas Eve, 1942. Included among De Leon's men were two French paratroopers who spoke Arabic and were familiar with the area, as well as five American demolition experts. To blow the bridge, 400 pounds of TNT would be dropped with the paratroopers.

Unknown to the paratroopers until morning, they had been dropped off course and had not reached the bridge. Therefore, with the mission compromised, they planted their explosives on a switching station and along the railway tracks, blowing these facilities as they split up to infiltrate back to the Allied lines. Some paratroopers were captured by the Italians, and then escaped; while De Leon and a few others hijacked an Italian truck and made it part way home before having to abandon the vehicle. Eventually, De Leon and seven others rejoined American forces, although others would escape later in the war. This proved to be the last airborne operation of the North African campaign as the men of the 509th fought as leg infantry until the end of hostilities.

While the airborne troops had been receiving their baptism of fire in North Africa, Airborne Command had continued its growth. In late October of 1942, the new glider training facility at Laurinburg-Maxton (about fifty miles from Fort Bragg) opened, with the 88th Glider infantry the first unit sent to the new post. Although this relieved the crowding at Fort Bragg slightly, the huge influx of troops for airborne training necessitated the activation of another base. Named Camp Mackell after a paratrooper killed in North Africa, this became the new home for Airborne Command.

Under the impetus of Eleanor Roosevelt, the Army had received pressure to create Negro combat units, so in February of 1943, the 555th Parachute Infantry Company (Colored) was formed with Black paratroopers, although the unit did not really start training until December of 1943. The "Triple Nickel" would provide the spawning ground of many of the Black paratroopers who would later play an important role in the 187th RCT in Korea and in the 82nd Airborne Division, 101st Airborne Division and Special Forces during the 1950s and 1960s.

February of 1943 also saw the activation of the 11th Airborne Division under MGEN Joseph Swing. Then two months later, the 17th Airborne Division was activated under MGEN William Miley. As these two new airborne divisions underwent their training, on 20 April 1943 the 82nd Airborne Division, forced to undergo the indignity of posing as "leg infantry," left Fort Bragg heading towards Camp Edwards, MA, then on to North Africa.

82nd Airborne troopers board a C-47 Skytrain prior to a jump in North Africa. Most of these troopers are armed with the .30 caliber M1 Garand semi-automatic rifle, the standard U.S. Army infantry rifle of the Second World War. (U.S. Army)

Included in the equipment being placed into an equipment container by this 82nd Airborne paratrooper is a mine detector, a field telephone set, .30 caliber ammunition belts, and a field barber set. (U.S. Army)

A "Stick" of 82nd Airborne paratroopers file onboard a C-47 Skytrain for a practice jump in North Africa. The last man in line carried an M1 Carbine, while the third man in line appears to be carrying an M1903 Springfield rifle. (U.S. Army)

Airborne Patches

82nd Airborne

101st Airborne

11th Airborne

17th Airborne

A pair of 82nd Airborne troopers prepare to pull themselves up on their risers just prior to landing. This technique helped lessen the impact and also lessened the chance of serious injury on landing. (U.S. Army)

An 82nd Airborne trooper gains control of his parachute during a practice jump in North Africa. The canopy is camouflaged with a multi-colored speckled pattern. (U.S. Army)

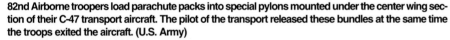

82nd Airborne troopers load parachute packs into special pylons mounted under the center wing section of their C-47 transport aircraft. The pilot of the transport released these bundles at the same time the troops exited the aircraft. (U.S. Army)

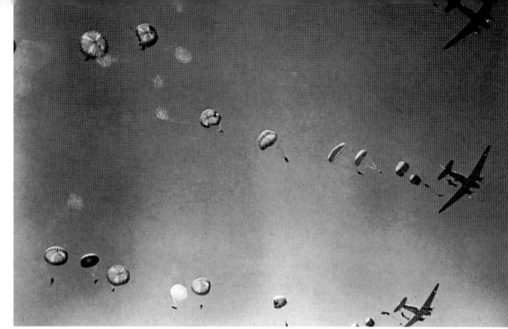

Sticks of 82nd Airborne paratroopers exit their Douglas C-47 Skytrain transport aircraft over North Africa. Most combat jumps by U.S. paratroopers were made from the C-47. (U.S. Army)

A very famous group of officers in North Africa during LTGEN George S. Patton's visit to the 82nd Airborne Division: Patton (left), MGEN Omar Bradley (center) MGEN Matthew Ridgway (Commander of the 82nd) and BGEN Maxwell Taylor (Commander of the 82nd Artillery, right). (U.S. Army)

11

82nd Airborne artillerymen tow a 75MM Pack Howitzer into position for loading onto a Waco CG-4A transport glider. The Pack Howitzer was the heaviest weapon available to the paratroops. (U.S. Army)

The small size of the Pack Howitzer allowed its four man crew to easily load the weapon into a glider without the aid of special equipment. Originally, the 75MM Pack Howitzer was designed for use by mountain troops. (U.S. Army)

Airborne artillerymen lift the nose of a Waco CG-4A to load a 75MM Pack Howitzer into the glider. The lift nose on the CG-4A allowed the airborne artillery to be brought into action very quickly once the glider landed. (U.S. Army)

Airborne troopers load a Jeep aboard a CG-4A glider. The White markings on the Jeep's bumper identify it belonging to the 82nd Airborne. (U.S. Army)

Airborne artillerymen are lashing their Pack Howitzer into position aboard a Waco glider. The loading ramp folded up to help secure the weapon in place. Any movement in flight could prove disastrous. (U.S. Army)

A Waco CG-4 glider is lifted off the runway by its tow aircraft, probably a Douglas C-47 Skytrain. The Waco CG-4 was the standard glider used by U.S. airborne troops during the Second World War. (U.S. Army)

Waco CG-4A Glider

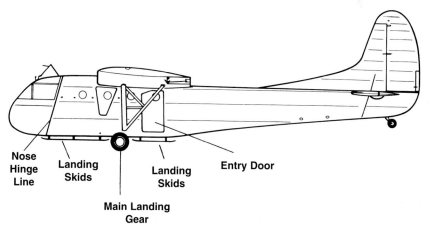

Nose Hinge Line

Landing Skids

Main Landing Gear

Landing Skids

Entry Door

Sicily

At the Casablanca Conference held in January of 1943, it was decided to try to knock Italy out of the war as soon as possible. As a result, it was determined that Sicily would be the next target for invasion by British/American forces in the ETO. To attempt to fool the Axis into expecting an attack elsewhere, British intelligence launched the famous "Man Who Never Was" disinformation operation by planting the body of an "officer" supposedly carrying plans for an invasion of Sardinia and Greece in Spain where German agents would be sure to receive the information. The Germans believed the ploy and increased security in both locations. Actually, on the night of 7 July, a couple of nights before the actual invasion of Sicily, six men of the British Special Air Service did jump onto Sardinia to attack an airfield, adding to the confusion of Axis intelligence.

As part of Operation HUSKY, as the Sicily invasion was code named, British and American airborne troops were slated to seize key road junctions and other terrain features. To accomplish these missions, there would be two British airborne landings and two American landings. To achieve surprise, the operations would be launched during the hours of darkness. The chief U.S. airborne advisor for the operation was MGEN Swing, called away while his 11th Airborne Division was undergoing training.

A British glider landing would begin the operation on the night of 9 July, followed by a jump by the 505th Parachute Regiment Combat Team under COL James Gavin about an hour later. The 505th's primary mission would be to block roads leading to the beachheads in order to slow the arrival of Axis reinforcements and to secure the Drop Zone (DZ) so that additional paratroopers of the 504th Parachute Infantry under COL Rueben Tucker could jump in the next night. Additionally, sixteen key pillboxes had to be neutralized. The final phase of the airborne operation would take place when the British jumped on the east coast of Sicily to seize the Primasole Bridge.

In preparation for the jump, the 82nd Airborne Division arrived in North Africa on 10 May 1943. Over the next seven weeks, the "All Americans" engaged in extremely strenuous combat training. To personally recon their drop zones, Gavin and two of his battalion commanders flew over Sicily to check for landmarks. Then, early in July, the paratroopers moved to various air bases.

As the men prepared for their jump on 9 July, the pilots of the 52nd Troop Carrier Wing were briefed on the very complex course they would have to fly to avoid detection. To complicate matters, weather conditions over the drop zones turned bad on 9 July, but Eisenhower decided that the operation would go ahead as planned. The presence of the large invasion armada had also alerted Italian intelligence to the possibility of invasion and the state of readiness of the troops on Sicily had been raised accordingly.

During their approach, the British gliders and their tow aircraft came under heavy anti-aircraft fire causing a number of the gliders to be cut loose too soon. As a result, many landed in the sea. In fact, only twelve gliders landed near their objective, but the glider troops still managed to capture it.

The men of the 505th Parachute Infantry also faced problems. Thirty-five mph winds were reported over the drop zones when they took off. Nevertheless, the operation remained a go. Many aircraft were blown off course, however, and as a result; most of the paratroopers were dropped well outside of their DZs. Many landed in the British invasion zone. Other aircraft were hit by anti-aircraft fire. As it turned out, only about an eighth of the paratroopers landed on their correct DZs. The others, even though scattered, did disrupt the enemy rear areas as they ambushed Axis patrols, cut telephone lines and made skillful nuisances of themselves. Other groups of paratroops attempted to carry out their missions, even though shorthanded. For example, about 100 paratroopers of the 1st Battalion,

505th Parachute Infantry under LTC Arthur Gorham blocked the Niscemi-Gela Road to prevent Axis reinforcements from reaching important strong points. The widely dispersed landings also had the effect of confusing Axis intelligence about where the actual landings would take place. Ironically, MAJ Mark Alexander's 2nd Battalion, 505th Parachute Infantry landed way off course but near some enemy pillboxes, which they captured thus greatly easing the 45th Infantry Division landings.

The cutting of communication lines by the scattered paratroopers also delayed Axis counter-attacks against the beachheads by disrupting communications. Although successfully blocking the Niscemi-Gela Road, COL Gorham was killed while engaging a German tank with a bazooka. The regimental commander, COL James Gavin, eventually gathered about 250 of his paratroopers and went into action against the Hermann Goering Panzer (Armored) Division to blunt its counter-attack against the beachheads. Despite heavy opposition, these men held Biazzo Ridge with the help of one of their 75MM Pack Howitzers, which engaged Tiger tanks.

On the night of 10 July, the 504th Parachute Infantry was ordered to jump on Farello Airstrip, which was held by the Americans. Since it appeared the drop zone would not be contested, the biggest worry was trigger-happy anti-aircraft gunners in the invasion armada and among the troops on the beachheads, since they had undergone heavy German and Italian air attacks throughout 10 July. Theoretically, however, all anti-aircraft units had been notified of the upcoming airborne operation.

The first transport aircraft arrived over their DZ at about 2240, shortly after the last enemy air attacks against the beachheads. Then, disaster struck as the second group of transports approached the drop zones. One anti-aircraft gunner opened up on the

An example of the equipment carried by a parachute mortarman during the invasion of Sicily. From top: main and reserve parachutes, 60MM M2 mortar bipod in its jump case, M1 Garand rifle, .45 caliber M1911 pistol, M3 Trench Knife, Model 1942 bayonet, and M1 grenades. Other equipment includes the M2 paratrooper's switchblade knife, an eighteen-inch machete, pistol magazine pouches, Garand clip pouches, rations and a compass. (U.S. Army)

transports and soon other itchy trigger fingers jerked in response. The sky over Sicily was filled with anti-aircraft fire; 23 of 144 USAAF transports were shot down by friendly fire and many others were badly damaged. There were a total of 318 American troops killed or wounded in the operation.

During the final stage of the airborne operation, British paratroopers jumped onto their DZ just as a group of German paratroopers descended on the same objective. As a result, vicious hand-to-hand combat resulted for control of the objective, with the British eventually securing the objective. Some of the British paratroopers had also died as a result of their aircraft being shot down by Allied anti-aircraft fire.

Once conventional troops had linked up with the paratroopers, the 82nd Airborne received heavy artillery support units allowing them to fight as conventional infantry during the advance up the coast of Sicily. Paratroopers saw action until the island was finally secured on 18 August.

The disastrous 504th encounter with Allied anti-aircraft gunners combined with the widely scattered 505th drop caused Eisenhower to order an investigative board. However, no blame was affixed in the anti-aircraft episode. Although the scattered drops had dissipated the airborne effort, it had still proven very successful in disrupting reinforcements. Eisenhower, however, recommended, as a result of the Sicily jumps, that the airborne divisions should be broken down into smaller more easily controllable units.

GEN Marshall took Eisenhower's recommendations seriously enough that he convened a special board under MGEN Joseph Swing to study the problem. After deliberation, this board recommended closer cooperation between Airborne Command and Troop Carrier Command, but the airborne divisions remained in the order of battle. Still, it was necessary to prove that an airborne division could be controlled in combat, so Swing's 11th Airborne Division carried out a highly successful demonstration maneuver to prove the point.

BGEN Maxwell Taylor of the 101st Airborne Division meets with Italy's Marshal Badoglio. BGEN Taylor did not go through parachute training and was not wearing parachute wings. He later received his wings for making a combat jump during the Normandy invasion. (U.S. Army)

A Jump on Rome – Almost

Shortly after the Allied landings on Sicily, high-ranking Italian Army officers began indicating a willingness to surrender to the Allies. At this point, Allied planners were pondering three possible moves after securing Sicily: (1) an attack across the Straits of Messina onto the toe of Italy, (2) an attack on the island of Sardinia and (3) an invasion of Corsica. It was decided that the attacks on the Italian mainland was the best move to knock Italy out of the war.

On 24 July 1943, the Fascist Grand Council voted to oust Mussolini and replace him with Marshall Pietro Badoglio. Distrustful, now that his friend Mussolini had been removed from power, Hitler ordered additional German troops to Italy. Meanwhile, the Allies had decided to land both on the toe of Italy and at Salerno. The British were scheduled to carry out landings on the toe on 3 September and drive northward, while the Americans would land at Salerno six days later. The 82nd Airborne Division was assigned to augment Mark Clark's forces during the operation. Initial plans called for the 82nd to make a combined parachute/glider assault. In preparation for this operation, on 20th August, the 82nd was ordered to North Africa where they worked on better coordination for night drops. The Krypton Lamp, which could give off a one second flash visible at 10,000 feet (even in daylight) was tested and pathfinder units were formed to jump in with this device ahead of major parachute forces.

However, rapidly changing conditions within the Italian government caused the 82nd's mission to be abruptly changed to an airborne mission to seize Rome itself. This change came about due to the Italian willingness to switch sides and out of fear of the 400,000 German troops now in Italy. The Italians did not want to switch sides until after the actual Allied landings and wanted an airborne division to drop on Rome to protect the King and Marshall Badoglio. The 82nd was slated to be that division. In return for this protection, Marshall Badoglio would announce an armistice before the actual Allied landings.

MGEN Ridgway was ordered to plan for a drop on Rome on 8 September, which was to be combined with amphibious landings and a major air landing operation. In the plan, the 504th and 505th Parachute Infantry regiments would jump and seize key air fields around Rome. Additional troops of the 82nd would then be flown into these airheads while heavier tank destroyer and other units would make an amphibious landing. However, due to the Italian unwillingness to fight the Germans, the operation was cancelled on the morning of 8 September after some aircraft had already taken off with their sticks of paratroopers.

Although the airborne operation had been called off, one small part, which had been launched in advance, was carried through. Forty-six men of the 509th Parachute Infantry had been sent to knock out the German radar station on the island of Ventotere to prevent detection of the approaching troop transports. 115 Germans were captured on the island even though the actual jump on Rome was called off. Under pressure from GEN Eisenhower, Badoglio agreed to an armistice before the landings as well.

At 0330 on 9 September, the amphibious landings at Salerno began. The Allied hold on the beachhead became tenuous when, on 12 September, the Germans launched a successful counter-attack. The situation became so critical that, on 13 September, GEN Mark Clark ordered the 82nd to prepare to drop directly onto the beachhead to reinforce the defense. As a result, Rueben Tucker's 504th Parachute Infantry took off at 1930 that evening and jumped onto the beachhead. The sight of the tough paratroopers floating down gave the defenders a morale boost as well as badly needed reinforcements. The next night another 1,900 paratroopers jumped in, to be followed by other 82nd units coming in over the beaches. The hard-fighting "All Americans" helped hold the beachhead and by 18 September the Germans withdrew, conceding the success of the landings.

The night of 14 September had seen another parachute operation, as members of the 509th Parachute Infantry Battalion jumped behind German lines near the town of Avellino, which lay astride a key road junction. This operation was designed to impede German reinforcements headed on for the beachhead. Due to Avellino's location in the mountains, the paratroopers had to jump from well over 4,000 feet. The mountains also made it very difficult to spot the beacons set up by the 509th pathfinders, which resulted in the drop being widely scattered. Although Ridgway had ordered LTC Doyle Yardley and his men to seize the crossroads at Avellino and hold them until the 5th Army could advance to meet them, this task would prove impossible since only ten sticks of paratroopers actually dropped near their assigned DZ. The secondary mission for the 509th, however, was to function as guerrillas. This mission was performed admirably. Throughout the night there were frequent firefights against German patrols. By the early morning of 15 September, LTC Yardley had gathered 160 of his men and was approaching Avellino, which it turned out was being held by a German panzer (armored) battalion. In the fighting around the town, Yardley and many of his paratroopers were taken prisoner. Other 509th members had better luck and one group of paratroopers linked up with Italian partisans and fought alongside them while another group blew up a bridge over which German reinforcements were passing.

The 5th Army breakout began on 23 September and as units advanced they kept meeting small groups of 509th paratroopers. As it turned out, the 509th, though unable to perform their primary mission had tied up numerous German units in searching for them, keeping these troops from attacking the beachhead.

After the Salerno landings, the 82nd Airborne was deployed to Scotland and, in early November, began to prepare for the upcoming landings in France. The 504th Parachute

LTC William Yarborough, Commander of the 509th Parachute Infantry, discusses plans for the upcoming invasion aboard HMS WINCHESTER CASTLE enroute to Anzio. LTC Yarborough wears the 509th pocket patch which he helped design. He also helped design the parachute wings and the jump uniform. (U.S. Army)

Infantry, however, along with attached engineer and artillery units were left with the 5th Army. The remnants of the 509th, now under COL William Yarborough, were honored by being assigned the duty guarding 5th Army HQ while it was brought back to full combat strength. The 509th, now veterans of multiple combat jumps, began the tradition of wearing combat jump stars on their parachute wings.

Anzio

To outflank the German defenses along the Gustav Line, an amphibious invasion at Anzio, about ten miles from Rome, was planned. This landing was to take place in conjunction with a frontal assault on the Gustav Line defenses. Assigned as part of the invasion force were the 504th Parachute Combat Team (PCT) – the 504th PIR, 376th Parachute Artillery Battalion and Company C, 307th Parachute Engineers – and the 509th Parachute Infantry Battalion. The 504th had been fighting as leg infantry during the advance towards Rome until pulled out of combat on 4 January 1944 to prepare for the Anzio operation. The 509th had been brought back up to full strength after the Avellino jump. Initially, it was planned to drop the 504th PCT behind the invasion beaches to seize key roads and bridges; however, it was decided that the paratroopers would land over the beach on 22 January with the rest of the invasion force. U.S. Rangers and the 509th PIB were assigned the mission of attacking into the heart of the city of Anzio.

As it turned out, the troops landed unopposed, although the Germans managed to establish a defensive shell around the beachhead when MGEN John Lucas (commander of the Anzio invasion forces) did not rapidly exploit the early success and break out of the beachhead. After three days, when Lucas was finally ready to push out of the beachhead, Field Marshal Kesselring, the German Commander in Italy, had managed to bring three divisions to oppose the beachhead. Even worse for the invaders, German artillery was now positioned on the high ground overlooking the beaches.

The 504th PCT was assigned to the right flank along the Mussolini Canal. From this position, on 24 January, they launched an attack to seize the town of Borgo Piave. Although successful, they were soon driven out by German tanks and artillery. They then held a defensive position along the canal until relieved on 28 January. After withdrawal, the 3rd Battalion, 504th PIR was assigned to the 1st Armored Division, while the remainder of the PCT was assigned to the 3rd Infantry Division. The 3/504th soon saw intensive combat fighting off a German counter-attack. As a result of this action, they became the first U.S. parachute unit to receive a Presidential Unit Citation.

Rejoined by the decimated 3rd Battalion, the 504th PCT was soon back in their defensive positions on the right flank where they carried out aggressive small unit infiltration patrols across the German lines. In response, the Germans named them the "Devils in Baggy Pants," a name proudly carried by the 504th from that time on.

The 509th PIB had been assigned to defend the point where the U.S. 3rd and 45th Infantry Divisions met. During one patrol out of this position, CPL Paul Huff won the first Congressional Medal of Honor awarded to a U.S. paratrooper.

On 22 February, Lucas was replaced by MGEN Lucian Truscott. Meanwhile, Hitler had ordered Kesselring to push the defenders of the Anzio beachhead into the sea and on 28 February, the Germans launched a massive assault against the beachhead. For their tenacious defense during this assault, the 509th PIB became the second parachute unit to win a Presidential Unit Citation.

In late March, the 504th PCT was withdrawn to England and assigned to the 82nd Airborne Division, while the 509th was withdrawn to prepare for the landings in the south of France, although its effective strength at this point was only 125 men. Finally in May, the Gustav Line was cracked and the stalemate at Anzio was broken as Allied troops advanced on both fronts, taking Rome on 4 June.

Night Drop Into Normandy

No one doubted that the invasions of North Africa, Sicily and Italy were just warmups for the upcoming landings in Western Europe. As initial planning for Operation OVERLORD progressed, it was envisioned that the airborne troops were to be inserted in company or, at most, battalion sized units to neutralize German shore batteries. As the invasion plan became more complex, however, it was decided to use three airborne divisions. At one point, GEN Marshall suggested dropping all three divisions on Paris with the drop to take place simultaneously with the amphibious landings. Although the idea of a rapid liberation of the French capital was certainly appealing, Eisenhower stressed that these troops might well be surrounded and slaughtered before they could be reinforced by heavier units. He also pointed out that they would be more useful helping to secure the beachhead.

To gain surprise, the airborne assaults were scheduled for the night before the amphibious landings. Not only would the cover of darkness help obtain surprise, it would also aid the airborne troops in creating confusion behind the German "Atlantic Wall." As initially formulated, the plan called for the British 6th Airborne Division to land on the eastern end of the beachhead, while the 82nd and 101st Airbornes would land on the western portion of the beachhead.

LTGEN Omar Bradley, commanding the U.S. invasion forces, planned to drop his airborne troops to seal the roads leading into the Cotentin Peninsula to block both German reinforcements and possible German escape routes. The 101st would land behind Utah Beach and seize the town of Sainte Mere-Eglise as well as knocking out costal guns and seizing crossings over the Merderet River. Once seized, they would hold until relieved by troops advancing out of the beachhead. Their mission would also include the seizure of four causeways leading from the beach. To beef up the 101st, the 501st Parachute Infantry was attached in January of 1944.

The 82nd Airborne was to drop about 20 miles inland from Utah Beach near Saint Sauveur le-Vicomte, which they would then have to hold until forces coming over the beaches linked up with them. For their D-Day missions, the 82nd had also been augmented by the 507th and 508th Parachute Infantry, in part to replace the 504th which had been detached in Italy. Additional reinforcements came to the 82nd and 101st in February of 1944 when a third battalion was added to each of their glider infantry regiments.

Intelligence estimates predicted that due to increased German anti-aircraft artillery, which had moved into the invasion area, casualties among airborne troops could run as high as 75%. Despite this estimate, it was decided to go ahead with the operation. Complicating training for the invasion were personnel changes in the upper command levels. In February of 1944, MGEN Bill Lee, the father of the airborne program and commander of the 101st Airborne, suffered a heart attack and had to be replaced by MGEN Maxwell Taylor, the Assistant Division Commander of the 82nd Airborne. Taylor, already combat experienced, drove his new charges in training, culminating in a full-scale exercise, Exercise EAGLE, held in May of 1944.

The Germans, expecting attack and under the able command of Field Marshal Erwin Rommel, had been beefing up their defenses including placing millions of *Rommel-spargel*, which were poles with mines on top, in open areas likely to attract airborne landings. In mid-May, Allied intelligence indicated another German division had moved into the Cotentin Peninsula. As a result, on 26 May, the plan was changed so both U.S. airborne divisions would jump just behind the beachhead. Most of the resulting changes, therefore, were in the 82nd's objective.

Paratroopers stand in the door of a C-47 during a practice jump prior to the Normandy invasion of June 1944. The crewman in the flying jacket is the aircraft's jump master. (IWM)

Paratroopers of the 101st Airborne Division, with their hair cut in a Mohawk style, apply war paint prior to the jump into Normandy. The paratrooper on the right appears to be wearing horsehide riding gauntlets, one of the types of gloves popular with airborne troops and is carrying an M1 Thompson Sub-Machine Gun (SMG). (U.S. Army)

Members of the 101st Airborne Division ready to board their transport prior to the airborne invasion of Normandy. Most of the troopers are armed with the M1 Garand rifles, except for the Bazookaman, who is carrying an M1 Carbine. (IWM)

M9A1 Rocket Launcher (Bazooka)

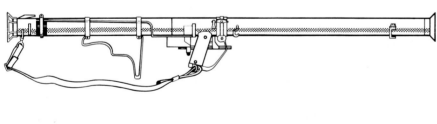

Folded For Jumping

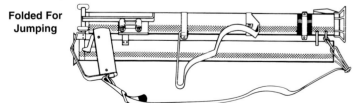

As finally developed, the plan called for three parachute landings and one glider landing by the 101st Airborne. The 502nd Parachute Infantry and the 377th Parachute Field Artillery would jump to secure the northernmost causeway, while the 506th Parachute Infantry would secure the two southernmost causeways. This left the 501st Parachute Infantry and Company C of the 326th Parachute Engineer Battalion to capture the locks over the Douve River at La Barquette to keep the Germans from blowing them and flooding the area. Once their objectives were secure, these units also had the mission of setting up defensive positions along the river. To follow up these parachute landings, 101st Airborne glider troops, especially artillery, anti-tank and signals units, would come in late on D-Day. The 327th Glider Infantry and the 1/401st Glider Infantry would come in over the beach, since there were not enough glider pilots trained to bring in all of the glider troops by air. In fact, many paratroopers had to act as co-pilots aboard gliders, their only training being On-the-Job Training (OJT) as they flew over the channel!

The final plan for the 82nd Airborne called for the 507th and 508th Parachute Infantry to establish defensive positions west of the Merderet River, while the 505th Parachute Infantry established positions east of the river. The primary mission for the 505th was the capture of the bridges at La Piere and Chef-du-Point as well as the capture of Sainte Mere-Eglise. Before dawn on D-Day, MGEN Ridgway planned to follow his paratroopers in with HQ, glider artillery, and signals just south of Sainte Mere-Eglise. They would be followed on D+1 by the 325th Glider Infantry and the 2/401st Glider Infantry. Although a smaller number of "All Americans" were scheduled to come in over the beaches, a small group of 325th Glider Infantrymen and glider artillerymen were to land along with a company from the 746th Tank Battalion and drive overland to link up with Ridgway's command post near Sainte Mere-Eglise.

On 5 June 1944, U.S. paratroopers began boarding their aircraft all over England. The plan called for the aircraft to approach at 1,500 feet to avoid as much anti-aircraft fire as possible, then descend to 500 feet for the drop. For those pilots who could not find their

A heavily ladened 82nd Airborne paratrooper, armed with a .45 Caliber M1 Thompson Sub-Machine Gun, boards his transport aircraft for the night jump into Normandy. The troops carried as many supplies as they could when making a combat jump. (IWM)

DZs, one DZ was designated as the alternate, but all paratroopers were to be dropped to create maximum disruption in the enemy rear. To attempt to insure accurate drops, eighteen aircraft loaded with pathfinders took off at 2300 on 5 June. The rest of the paratroopers began taking off around 0030 on 6 June. Pathfinders from the 101st began landing at 0015, though most were off course. Their comrades and friendly rivals of the 82nd had little that they would later be able to brag about either, since they were also off course. As a result of the scattering of the pathfinders combined with heavier anti-aircraft fire than anticipated and inexperienced pilots, the drops into France were widely scattered. Making things even more difficult were the darkness and the thick hedgerows, which impeded the paratroopers as they tried to assemble into cohesive fighting units.

As the first sticks dropped in, the 101st Airborne had faced less anti-aircraft fire than the following 82nd Airborne and were less scattered, although they still faced massive re-assembly difficulties. Despite being widely scattered, however, members of the "All Americans" pushed towards their objectives, often in small groups. The 3/505th rapidly seized Sainte Mere-Eglise. The men of the 2/505th also moved rapidly towards their objective, Neuville-au-Plain, despite the fact that their commander LTC Ben Vandervoort had suffered a broken foot during the drop. Vandervoort, however, was ordered to stop short of his objective since the regimental commander did not know if the 3/505th had been successful in securing Sainte Mere-Eglise. The loss of radios during the jump complicated command and control throughout the operations by the paratroopers in Normandy.

At that point, Sainte Mere-Eglise was in American hands, but at 0930 on 6 June the Germans launched a counter-attack. As a result, all but one platoon of the 2/505th were sent to reinforce the 3/505th. Meanwhile, that lone platoon under LT Turner Turnbull marched into Nueville-au-Plain to hold the road leading to Sainte Mere-Eglise. As it turned out, this proved to be a key blocking position as the platoon fought off an attack by a German infantry regiment for four hours, preventing them from reaching Sainte Mere-Eglise.

The toughest time of all, however, for the battalions of the 505th was faced by the 1/505th. This battalion's objective was the bridge at La Piere over the Merderet. Despite three assaults, the battalion was unable to dislodge the defenders. Eventually, BGEN James Gavin, who had landed off course near La Piere, gathered a group of about 300 paratroopers and tried to help force the crossing. He split his force, sending half to seize the bridge at Chef-du-Pont, while he kept the other half for action against the La Piere bridge. After a hard fight, the Chef-du-Pont bridge was taken, but it took CAPT Ben Schwartzwaler (later a famous football coach at Syracuse) with elements of the 507th Parachute Infantry to eventually push across. They continued advancing to link up with the rest of the badly scattered 507th allowing the Germans to retake the bridge and hold it for two more days.

.45 Caliber M1 Thompson SMG

Troopers of Battery C, 377th Parachute Artillery, 101st Airborne Division, prepare their Pack Howitzers for dropping prior to the Normandy Invasion. The cases were then slung under the C-47 and dropped when the troops dropped. (U.S. Army)

Glider troops of the 101st Airborne Division on board a Waco CG-4 glider. These men are armed with a variety of weapons including: M1 Garand rifles, a .45 caliber M1 Thompson sub-machine gun, a Browning Automatic Rifle (BAR), and a Bazooka. (U.S. Army)

The 508th Parachute Infantry was also badly scattered, but not as badly as the 507th. The 508th's primary objectives were the bridges over the Douve River. One lieutenant of the 508th made a good start by killing the German general commanding the 91st Infantry Division. Another especially important operation by paratroopers of the 2/508th led by LTC Thomas Shanley was the defense of Hill 30 against repeated German attacks. By holding, Shanley and his men prevented the Germans from rolling up other groups of paratroopers and putting the airhead in jeopardy.

In the 101st area, LTC Richard Cole, commander of the 3/502nd, landed miles from the causeways, which were his battalion's objective, but he gathered a mixed force and marched to the objectives, occupying them without opposition. Other causeways and two bridges to the south of the airhead were the objectives of the 506th Parachute Infantry, which was also badly scattered. The 3/506th had been decimated during the jump when they had the misfortune of jumping into an area identified by German intelligence as a very likely drop zone. As a result, the Germans had turned it into a killing ground with artillery and machine guns pre-zeroed. With the 3/506th out of contact with COL Sink, the regimental commander, he grew more and more worried about their fate.

Maxwell Taylor, the 101st C.O. had sent his reserve battalion, the 3/501st, against the causeways as well. Although they encountered heavy fighting they were successful in securing their objective. The remainder of the 501st landed on their correct DZ and, after moderate fighting, seized the key river lock at La Barquette.

At about 0400 on D-Day, American Waco gliders began arriving, many crashing into obstacles while landing. Seventeen hours later, the larger Horsas were scheduled to come in. Without confirmation from the 82nd HQ that the LZ was totally secure, the decision was taken in England to send the Horsas in an hour earlier than planned to gain an extra bit of daylight. This made a complicated situation even more difficult, as airborne troops and members of the 4th Infantry Division, expecting a landing at 2100, were still trying to clear the LZs as the gliders began coming in. Fortunately, many overshot the LZ, while others landed under fire. The LZ was finally secured by troops under LTC Edson Raff around 0700 on D+1 just as the 325th Glider Infantry began arriving.

.45 Caliber Colt M1911A1 Pistol

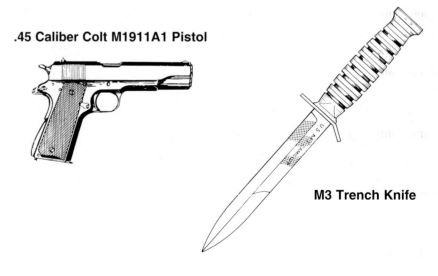

M3 Trench Knife

By daylight on 8 June, the 82nd Airborne Division was in control of its objectives and was mopping up remaining resistance. However, the bridge at La Piere remained in German hands. To finally wrest control of this important crossing, glider troops crossed the Merderet on a submerged bridge and attacked the Germans from the rear. In this operation, PFC Charles De Glopper won a posthumous Congressional Medal of Honor. It was not, however, until a combined attack by the 2/325th and 2/401st Glider Infantry Battalions supported by a heavy artillery barrage, that the bridge was finally cleared of its tenacious German defenders.

By D+3 most airborne objectives had been secured, often by units other than those initially assigned the objective. Both divisions had suffered heavy casualties, although nowhere near to the extent predicted. Each had about 1,200 listed as killed, wounded or missing. Despite their scattered drops, the airborne troops had saved the lives of many infantrymen coming across the beaches by occupying German troops who might have counter-attacked or by knocking out shore batteries. Although the flooding and hedgerows had hindered movement by the paratroopers, they had also inhibited German counter-attacks.

Once its objectives were secured, the 82nd Airborne continued to fight west as leg infantry to cut off the Cotentin Peninsula, both to bottle up retreating German troops and prevent reinforcements from reaching their comrades. The 101st Airborne, on the other hand, fought south to take the city of Carentan, but they only gained control of their objective after a three day battle, then had to fight off a German counter-attack. By the second week of July, with the Allied position on the continent of Europe secure, the 82nd and 101st Airborne Divisions were pulled back to England, having suffered almost 10,000 casualties between them during the weeks of fighting in France.

82nd Airborne armorers check weapons prior to a supply drop into Normandy. The two men wearing side caps both wear the paraglider badge. Among the weapons being serviced are a Browning Automatic Rifle (BAR), M1 Garands and a .30 Caliber Browning M1919 air-cooled Machine Gun. (U.S. Army)

A paratrooper, who has just landed in Normandy, releases himself from his parachute and prepares to go into action. He carries an M3 Trench Knife strapped to his right calf, a .45 caliber M1911A1 semi-automatic pistol on his hip, and a dispatch case worn over the pistol. (IWM)

21

C-47 transports towing British Horsa gliders loaded with supplies pass over Utah Beach on 6 June 1944 on their way to resupply the airborne troops battling further inland. (U.S. Army)

C-47 Skytrain

Horsa Glider

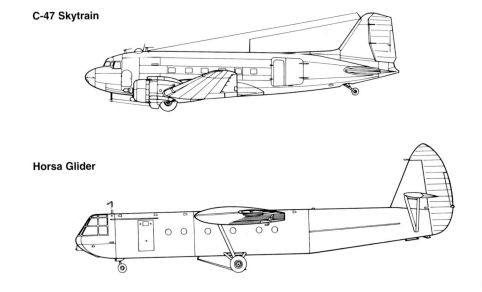

An 82nd Airborne paratrooper, his shoulder sleeve insignia obscured by a wartime censor, enjoys a liberated bottle of wine with a medic during a lull in operations after the jump into occupied France. The medic has liberated a German officer's hat and German flag. (IWM)

Members of the 101st Airborne, along with a French liaison officer, move through a liberated French city during combat operations after the airborne invasion of France. Most of these troops are armed with M1 Carbines. (IWM)

A Major of the 502nd Parachute Infantry escorts a captured German officer in for interrogation. The paratrooper officer has a regimental insignia on his jacket. (IWM)

Operation ANVIL: Airborne Operations In Southern France

In August of 1943, it was decided to launch Operation ANVIL, the invasion of Southern France, before Operation OVERLORD. The slowness of the Allied advance in Italy, however, put a hold on the operation in April of 1944. Once Operation OVERLORD had been launched and the Allies had successfully invaded Normandy, Eisenhower pushed once again for Operation ANVIL to be carried out with two primary objectives – the seizure of the port of Marseilles and the tying down of the maximum number of Germans to keep them out of the drive across northern France. Reportedly because Churchill felt he had been "dragooned" into accepting the operation, its name was changed to Operation DRAGOON and set for 15 August.

The U.S. VI Corps under LTGEN Lucian Truscott was the prime invasion unit. Included in this corps was the 1st Airborne Task Force, a division-sized unit including the British 2nd Independent Parachute Brigade, the U.S. 509th Parachute Infantry Battalion

American paratroopers display a captured German flag and helmet taken during operations in France. The trooper standing next to the flag (left) carries three Mk 11A1 fragmentation grenades and an unidentified smooth grenade suspended from his harness. (U.S. Army)

(Reinforced), the 517th Parachute Combat Team (517th Parachute Infantry, 460th Parachute Field Artillery, and 590th Airborne Engineer Company), the 550th Glider Infantry Battalion and the 551st Parachute Infantry Battalion. In command was MGEN Robert T. Frederick, former commander of the 1st Special Service Force. Additional units attached to the 517th Parachute Combat Team included a Japanese-American anti-tank company from the 442nd Regimental Combat Team and Company D, 83rd Chemical Mortar Battalion with 4.2 inch mortars. Both of these units would go in aboard gliders.

The invasion plan called for the 1st Airborne Task Force to jump around Le Muy just before dawn on 15 August to block German reinforcements from reaching the beachheads. VI Corps would secure the beaches and be ready to move northwest, while the French I and II Corps would follow through the beachhead to strike towards Toulon and Marseilles.

Frederick's plan for the airborne operation would send pathfinders in at 0330 followed by additional parachute elements an hour later. Their mission would be to seize towns and roads in key block positions around the beachhead. Some gliderborne troops would come in at 0800. On the afternoon of D-Day, the 551st Parachute Infantry would arrive by parachute and the 550th Glider Infantry by glider.

Once again the pathfinders were misdropped, but ironically a larger percentage of the paratroopers were still dropped on their correct DZs. Three aircraft loads of the 509th Parachute Infantry and two aircraft loads of the 463rd Parachute Field Artillery who were dropped off course linked up with French Forces and helped liberate Saint Tropez.

All aspects of the operation seemed to go well and, by noon on D-Day, VI Corps had their beachhead well established, while the airborne units had occupied almost all of their objectives around the beachhead. The 1/517th, however, was still sharing control of Les Arcs with the Germans. The arrival of the 551st PIB and 550th GIB, allowed Les Arcs to be cleared. Early on D+1, the town of Le Muy was taken by a mixed force from the 1st Airborne Task Force, with 700 Germans surrendering. Also on D+1, the 551st Parachute Infantry captured Draguignan where they took personnel of a German corps HQ prisoner.

With the operation an obvious success, the paratroopers were relieved by the evening of D+1. Exploiting his rapid achievement of the invasion objectives, Truscott drove out of the beachhead in an attempt to trap the retreating German 19th Army. Although not all were cut off, 57,000 Germans were captured.

The 1st Airborne Task Force, meanwhile, was given the mission of covering the 7th Army's right flank, in the process liberating the Riviera including Nice and Cannes. Their advance finally stopped when they occupied positions in the Maritime Alps. The combination of the easy advance and the move along the Riviera caused this operation to be called the "Champagne Campaign." Once in their defensive positions, the 1st Airborne Task Force guarded the Maritime Alps through mid-September. On 18 September, they began expanding their position, but in October the airborne units were relieved and the 1st Airborne Task Force was disbanded at the end of November.

A LT of the 101st Airborne dressed in service dress "Pinks." His decorations include the glider badge, Combat Infantryman Badge and ribbons for the Bronze Star, Purple Heart and Europe-Africa-Middle East Campaign.

A trooper of the 501st Parachute Infantry Battalion wears the early balloon satin jump suit and A2 cloth helmet. He is equipped with a T-4 parachute and early pattern jump boots.

MGEN James Gavin, commander of the 82nd Airborne Division, prepares for a practice jump during 1945. He is dressed in a B-10 Flying Jacket and leather gloves along with a T-7 parachute with quick release for the parachute harness. MGEN Gavin normally jumped with the first sticks during combat.

A member of the 11th Airborne Division on occupation duty in Japan. He is armed with a folding stock M1A1 Carbine and carries a canteen and magazine pouch suspended from an M1936 belt.

This member of the 17th Airborne Division during Operation Varsity wears an M1943 Field Uniform and M1943 jump boots. He is armed with an M1 Garand rifle and M3 Trench Knife strapped to his leg.

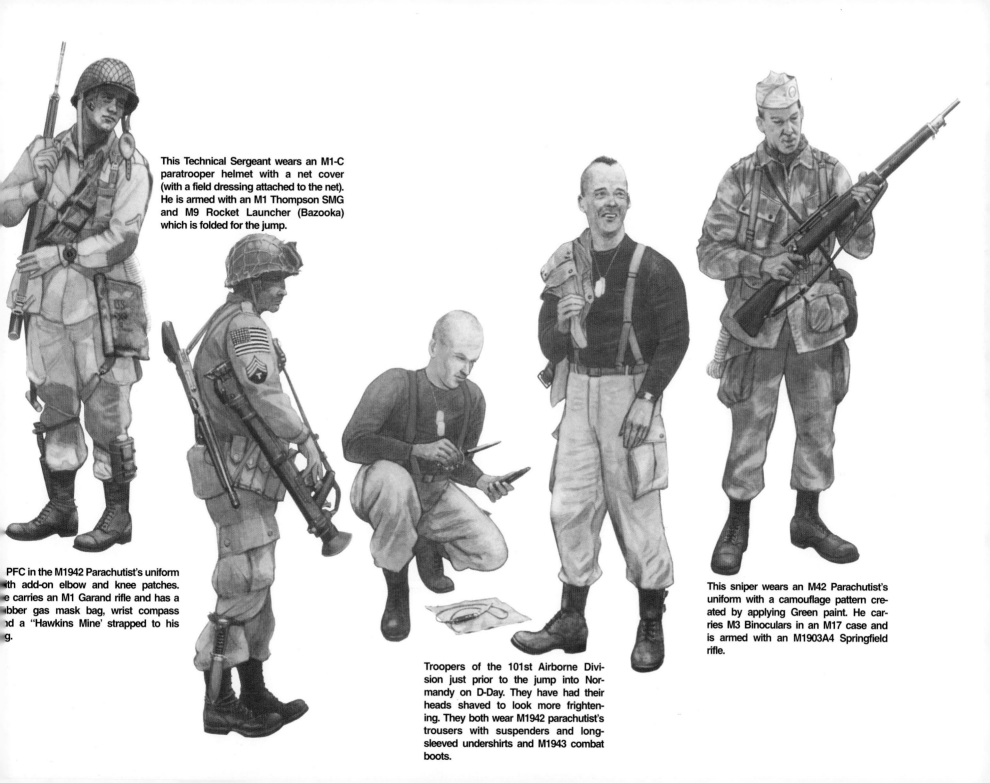

This Technical Sergeant wears an M1-C paratrooper helmet with a net cover (with a field dressing attached to the net). He is armed with an M1 Thompson SMG and M9 Rocket Launcher (Bazooka) which is folded for the jump.

PFC in the M1942 Parachutist's uniform ith add-on elbow and knee patches. e carries an M1 Garand rifle and has a bber gas mask bag, wrist compass d a "Hawkins Mine' strapped to his g.

Troopers of the 101st Airborne Division just prior to the jump into Normandy on D-Day. They have had their heads shaved to look more frightening. They both wear M1942 parachutist's trousers with suspenders and long-sleeved undershirts and M1943 combat boots.

This sniper wears an M42 Parachutist's uniform with a camouflage pattern created by applying Green paint. He carries M3 Binoculars in an M17 case and is armed with an M1903A4 Springfield rifle.

Operation MARKET GARDEN

As the Allies, led by Patton's Third Army, broke out into France and the German defenses began to crumble, Field Marshal Montgomery suggested a plan to rapidly drive through Belgium and Holland into Germany. This plan, however, would have brought the American drive on Germany virtually to a stand still so Ike approved a compromise plan, which would allow Montgomery's 21st Army Group to push on to Antwerp to seize the important port. Simultaneously, Omar Bradley's 12th Army Group would continue to advance toward the Rhine.

On 2 August 1944, the 1st Allied Airborne Army was activated to bring the U.S. XVIIIth Airborne Corps, British airborne troops, and air transport assets under one command. The staff of the 1st AAA immediately began planning various operations to seize critical objectives ahead of the advancing Allied armies, but so rapid was the advance that these objectives were overrun each time before the operation could be implemented. 1st Allied Airborne Army's chance came on 9 September, when Montgomery proposed Operation MARKET GARDEN, a combined airborne/ground operation to cut off retreating Germans and secure a bridgehead across the Rhine.

The plan called for airborne troops to seize a "carpet" of five bridges and the roads linking them ahead of an armored spearhead. The highest-ranking airborne officer on the 1st AAA staff, LTGEN Frederick Browning, however, felt that the airborne penetration was too deep considering there was only one road along which the armored thrust would take place. As a result he coined his famous comment that they were going "a bridge too far." Nevertheless, the operation was a "go" and would be launched on 17 September 1944. Browning decided that three and a half airborne divisions would be needed to carry out the operation. As a result, the U.S. 82nd Airborne, U.S. 101st Airborne, British 1st Airborne, and Polish 1st Parachute Brigade were given the mission.

The British 1st Airborne Division drew the furthest bridge at Arnhem as their assignment, since they had previously planned for a mission in this area. On D+2 they would be reinforced by the Polish 1st Parachute Brigade. Seizing the middle portion of the carpet would be the 82nd Airborne Division as they were assigned to capture bridges over the Maas and Waal and some heights, which overlooked the area. The 101st Airborne's mission was to seize and hold the bridges and roads nearest to the Allied tanks, which were to dash to relieve them. This was a change from the original plan, since the 101st had been originally slated to carry out the Arnhem jump. Even in these early planning stages many felt that the British planned to jump too far from their objectives at Arnhem as they would have a two-hour march to the bridge. The plans, however, were not changed.

In Gavin's 82nd Airborne, the 504th Parachute Infantry had replaced the 507th Parachute Infantry, which was now assigned to the newly arrived 17th Airborne Division. Since the 82nd's mission was to first seize the Groesbeek Heights, then the Nijmegen Bridge, Gavin planned to drop the 505th and 508th Parachute Infantry and the 376th Parachute Field Artillery east of the Heights to seize and occupy them. The 508th Parachute Infantry would seize and hold a DZ for the 325th Glider Infantry, which would be reinforcing the paratroopers on D+1, then secure the Groesbeek Heights prior to helping the 504th Parachute Infantry capture two bridges across the Maas-Waal Canal. Finally, they would assist in capturing the five-span Nijmegen Bridge across the Waal. The 505th Parachute Infantry had the mission of taking the town of Groesbeek and defending the base of the heights, while the 37th PFA would give supporting fire in case

MGEN James Gavin, commander of the 82nd Airborne Division, moves among his paratroopers of the 508th Parachute Infantry. "Jumpin' Jim" Gavin has supplemented his .45 pistol with an M1 Garand since he was operating close to the enemy. MGEN Gavin commanded the 82nd during Operation MARKET GARDEN and the drive into Germany. (U.S. Army)

BGEN James "Jumpin' Jim" Gavin, Commanding General of the 82nd Airborne Division, prepares his gear for Operation MARKET GARDEN on 17 September 1944. Airborne generals were unusual in that they carried rifles in addition to the standard .45 caliber sidearm. (U.S. Army)

of a German counter-attack. To put them nearer their objectives, the 504th would drop west of the Groesbeek Heights and capture the nine-span Waal River Bridge and three other bridges over the Maas-Waal Canal. The 508th's portion of this mission was to assist with the capture of the bridge nearest to Nijmegen. One company would be dropped on the opposite side of the Maas so that the large bridge could be attacked from both sides.

In the 101st, Taylor planned to drop all of his parachute units into two DZs from which they could seize control of fifteen miles of "Hell's Highway." The 506th Parachute Infantry would take the bridge over the Wilhelmina Canal and secure Eindhoven, while the 501st Parachute Infantry would take the bridges over the Waal River and Wilhelmina Canal.

Unknown to the Allies was the fact that the Germans had sent the 9th and 10th SS Panzer Divisions to Arnhem to refit. The German 1st Parachute Army had also been sent to Holland. These moves did not go completely unnoticed by Allied intelligence, although the extent of German reinforcements was not known. As a result, Eisenhower suggested that another airborne division be dropped at Arnhem or that the two American divisions be dropped further south, but Montgomery rejected the suggestion.

On the night before the massive drop in Holland, Allied bombers saturated German airfields anywhere near the DZs and hit German AA all along the coast of Holland on the morning of D-Day. Despite this massive preparatory bombing, the Germans were still caught by surprise as the 1,545 troop carrier planes, 478 gliders and 1,130 fighter escorts roared overhead. The 82nd lost a few of their transport aircraft to flak, but it was the 101st Airborne that suffered the most heavy losses and damage to aircraft since the transports of the 82nd Airborne and 1st Airborne, which had passed over initially had alerted the defenders. A total of 68 transports, gliders and fighters were lost, but scattering was minimal and MARKET GARDEN proved the most accurate drop of the war so far, much of the success being attributable to it being a daylight drop.

The 501st PIR of the 101st Airborne rapidly seized their objectives along "Hell's Highway," while the 502nd, after securing most of their objectives, were stopped short of Best. The 506th PIR also ran into heavy resistance allowing the Germans time to blow the Zon road bridge, thus preventing the 506th from reaching Eindhoven.

In the 82nd area, the 504th PIR quickly took the nine-span bridge over the Maas River by hitting both ends simultaneously, thus securing one of the most important D-Day objectives. The 505th also was successful in taking the town of Groesbeek relatively easily. Once it was secured, they set up positions facing the Reichswald to prepare for an expected counter-attack. Although the 508th PIR was successful in cutting the wires to blow up the Nijmegen Bridge, preventing the Germans from destroying it, they could not take the bridge due to heavy German resistance. This resistance would soon get worse since the 9th SS was sent to oppose the British at Arnhem, while the 10th SS was sent to Nijmegen to defend the bridge over the Waal.

The situation at Arnhem was already bad and getting worse. MGEN Roy Urquhart, the commander of the 1st Airborne had not sent his troops toward Arnhem for four hours after landing thus allowing the 9th SS time to arrive and get into position. As a result, when the British airborne troops started their advance to the objective they ran into heavy fire. The 3rd Battalion, under LTC John Frost, did manage to make it into Arnhem and even got one company near the bridge controlling the north end. The heroic stand of Frost's men near the bridge would become legendary, but they did not take the objective.

By the end of D-Day, things were not going all that well in the American divisional zones either. The 101st still had not taken Eindhoven, while the 82nd had not secured the Nijmegen Bridge. By D+1, however, the 506th PIR of the 101st had captured the

Eindhoven bridges over the Dommel River. Nevertheless, the spearhead of British tanks did not reach them until 1900 that night. D+1 also saw the reinforcement of the 101st Airborne by the arrival of the 327th Glider Infantry. During the night of D+1, British engineers threw a bridge across the Wilhelmina Canal so that the advance on Nijmegen could continue; however, the 82nd still had not secured the Nijmegen Bridge.

Just before the glider-borne reinforcements for the 82nd were to land on D+1, the Germans struck at the glider LZ from the Reichswald. Just prior to the gliders being released, members of the 508th PIR managed to clear the Germans from the LZ allowing the 325th GIR and the glider artillery to land safely, or as safely as glider-borne troops could ever land. On the morning of D+2, British tanks reached the 82nd's 504th PIR, which still left them far short of relieving the hard-pressed British airborne troops at Arnhem.

LTGEN Lewis Brereton, the commander of the 1st Allied Airborne Army, and LTGEN Matthew Ridgway, commander of the XVIIIth Airborne Corps, arrived in Eindhoven on D+2 and immediately got separated in the fighting, not to find each other again until they were back in the UK. The 82nd, meanwhile, was still held up at the Nijmegen Bridge; therefore, when Horrocks reached Gavin's command post, they decided to launch a combined assault on the bridge using assault boats so that elements of the 82nd could outflank the defenders. Unfortunately, the assault boats would not be available for some twenty-four hours. Nevertheless, the 2/505th, under LTC Ben Vandervoort, and attached British infantry and tanks prepared to assault the bridge immediately, but they were pinned by heavy German fire.

Assigned to carry out the assault crossing of the Maas the next afternoon was the 504th PIR, their mission critical since the bridge had to be taken before the tanks could advance to relieve the British airborne troops at Arnhem. While the "All Americans" (82nd ABN) were moving into position for the crossing, the Germans attempted another counterattack out of the Reichswald but were beaten back.

MGEN Maxwell Taylor, Commanding General of the 101st Airborne Division, checks his harness prior to boarding the C-47 for Operation MARKET GARDEN. General Taylor earned his jump wings by making combat jumps rather than going through jump training at Fort Benning. (U.S. Army)

Field grade officers of the 82nd Airborne are briefed on their various objectives for Operation MARKET GARDEN. The briefing officer would go over the plan for the operation in detail using maps and photographs. (U.S. Army)

With tank and artillery fire support, the first wave of 504th paratroopers, in twenty-six assault boats, began their assault crossing under withering fire. After suffering 200 casualties during the heavy fighting, they finally seized the north side of the bridge at 1900. Having sacrificed many of their buddies in the crossing, the paratroopers of the 504th began to grow angry as the British tanks did not immediately roar across the bridge. At dawn on D+4, the 504th solidified their hold on the bridge, then had to fight off a German counterattack just before noon, PVT John Towle winning a Congressional Medal of Honor in the process. Still, the tanks did not move. In fact it was not until D+5 that British armored forces moved on toward Arnhem.

While the 82nd was mopping up around their objectives, the 101st found itself battling to hold open "Hells Highway", which the Germans had cut on D+5. In fact, it was not until D+9 that the "Screaming Eagles" regained total control.

Although the 1st Polish Parachute Brigade jumped on D+4, they could not break through from their DZs on the opposite side of the Lower Rhine. Finally on 24 September, the order was given for the 1st Airborne Division to withdraw, but 7,000 British airborne troops had become casualties in the operation. Although they had not suffered as heavily as their red-bereted comrades, the American airborne had taken over 3,500 casualties as well.

To make the best of the situation and hold what ground they had taken, the 82nd took up positions on the south side of the Lower Rhine, while the 101st Airborne tightened their hold on "Hell's Highway." The 101st then moved past the 82nd to take up new positions, encountering some heavy fighting in the process. Both U.S. airborne divisions continued to fight as "leg" infantry for the next two months, suffering another 3,500 casualties in the process.

When the 82nd and 101st were finally pulled back, they were both assigned billets around Rheims where some of the units which had taken part in Operation DRAGOON joined them as reinforcements and replacements. The XVIIIth Airborne Corps now consisted of the 17th Airborne Division, 82nd Airborne Division, 101st Airborne Division, 509th Parachute Infantry Battalion, 551st Parachute Infantry Battalion, and 463rd Parachute Field Artillery Battalion. Although the paratroopers could finally get a little leave time, as Christmas 1944 approached, Adolf Hitler and the *Oberkommando der Wehrmacht* (OKW; German Armed Forces High Command) had other plans for them.

Paratroopers of the 82nd Airborne Division board their C-47 Skytrain transport for Operation MARKET GARDEN during September of 1944. All of these troopers are carrying .45 caliber M1911 semi-automatic pistols. (U.S. Army)

The CG-4 Waco glider was used to deliver both glider troops and supplies during Operation MARKET GARDEN. This operation was made famous by the quote of LTGEN Frederick Browning, who said that the British airborne forces were going "a bridge too far." (USAF)

"NUTS!" To The Ardennes Offensive

In September of 1944, Hitler decided that an offensive to take Antwerp depriving the Allies of a critical harbor, would force an Anglo-American withdrawal from the continent. For this offensive, twenty-nine divisions were secretly built up behind the Siegfried Line. Two of the initial key objectives of the German offensive would be the towns of Bastogne and St. Vith, both of which were astride key road junctions. Once these objectives were taken, the German Panzers (armored forces) could then drive on to Antwerp. Originally, the strike through the Ardennes was scheduled for November, but Operation MARKET GARDEN pushed it back to December. In actuality, this proved a fortuitous decision for the Germans since the cold and the approach of Christmas caused the Allies to drop their guard slightly. Since a German counterattack was unexpected, particularly through the Ardennes, this area was lightly held by the under-strength U.S. VII Corps.

At 0530 on 16 December, the offensive began with early successes against the Americans all along the front. As the Panzers overran the thinly held front, the only reserves available were the 82nd and 101st Airborne Divisions. With LTGEN Ridgway at a meeting in the UK, "Jumping Jim" Gavin was in temporary command of the XVIIIth Airborne Corps as well as his own 82nd Airborne Division. MGEN Taylor of the 101st was also away representing the XVIIIth Airborne corps at a meeting in Washington, while his deputy commander was also away in the UK. As a result, temporary command of the 101st Airborne had fallen on the divisional artillery commander, BGEN Anthony

McAuliffe. With the situation worsening on the evening of the 17th, both airborne divisions were ordered to move towards Bastogne.

Meanwhile, LTGEN Ridgway rushed back to the continent to rejoin his troops, but before leaving England he ordered the 17th Airborne to prepare for immediate deployment to Europe. Gavin, still in command of the XVIIIth Airborne Corps until Ridgway's arrival, reached 1st Army HQ on the morning of 18 December. According to his orders, the 82nd Airborne was to be attached to V Corps north of Bastogne near Werbomont, while the 101st Airborne was assigned the defense of Bastogne. Ridgway arrived in Werbomont on the night of 18 December, allowing Gavin to concentrate on getting the "All Americans" into their defensive positions by the morning of 19 December. Simultaneously, the 101st had established their defensive positions around Bastogne.

On the morning of the 19 December, the Germans cut the road links between the 82nd and 101st positions as the offensive flowed around the paratroopers. By the 20th, Bastogne and St. Vith were surrounded but their tenacious defense was holding up the German advance. Various fragments of other shattered units had joined the 101st around Bastogne too, rallying to defend what was becoming the primary stumbling block to the Germans.

On 22 December, the Germans were confident enough to ask McAuliffe to surrender Bastogne, to which he gave his now famous reply – "Nuts!". Patton's Third Army had

101st Airborne Artillery Commander BGEN McAuliffe (right) was the author of the famous "Nuts" reply to the German request for surrender at Bastogne. He has the White circle recognition device painted on his helmet (artillery) while the unidentified BGEN to his left has a square symbol indicating divisional HQ. (U.S. Army)

Members of the 101st Airborne Division return from a night skirmish on New Year's Eve, 1944. The bitter cold and snow helped the Germans during the Battle of the Bulge by keeping Allied aircraft grounded. These troopers carry sleeping bags, blankets, canteen cups and boxes of rations. (U.S. Army)

already started their drive to cut off the German "Bulge" in the Allied lines, although it would take until 26 December to finally lift the siege of Bastogne. Nevertheless, the Screaming Eagles warranted McAuliffe's confidence in them as they held against ground, air and artillery pounding.

The 82nd Airborne also faced a difficult struggle to hold their positions along the northern edge of the German penetration. Gavin's seasoned paratroopers held their line so the forces which had been defending St. Vith could retreat through them. The 504th PIR faced particularly heavy German attacks, winning their second Presidential Unit Citation in the process.

On the 82nd's right flank, the 509th Parachute Infantry and 517th Parachute Combat Team were attached to the 3rd Armored Division. PFC Melvin Biddle won the Congressional Medal of Honor during these operations to eliminate German resistance in the town of Hotton. Alongside, elements of the 3rd Armored, the 509th PIB and 1/517th held a seven-mile front from 22-30 December against constant attacks from the 2nd SS Panzer Division. Once again the 509th was decimated in a heroic defense, winning their second Presidential Unit Citation.

So heavy was the fighting in the sections held by the airborne troops, that Ridgway himself had to make use of his 1903A3 Springfield rifle to kill three Germans in a vehicle.

On 27 December, the 9th SS Panzer Division and the 62nd Volks Grenadier Division launched a last-ditch attack against the 82nd Airborne. The paratroopers and glider riders hung tough, though, and the 3/508th even allowed German tanks to roll over their dug-in positions then counterattacking them from the rear and driving them off.

The German thrust blunted on 3 January 1945, the Allies began an offensive to eliminate the "Bulge" from the north. The 82nd Airborne was in the forefront of this advance. In the process, airborne troops would frequently still stumble upon parties of Germans resulting in a confusing melee. In one such encounter, 1SGT Leonard Funk,

An M24 Chaffee light tank assigned to the 740th Tank Battalion, 82nd Airborne Division in a Belgian town during January of 1945. The M24 weighed twenty tons and had a 75MM main gun. (U.S. Army)

The crew of a 75MM Pack Howitzer sight in on a German target during the Battle of the Bulge. This weapon was the largest gun normally available to airborne artillerymen during the war. (U.S. Army)

already one of the most heavily decorated soldiers in the Army, won a Congressional Medal of Honor for preventing his unit being taken prisoner.

The 82nd continued its advance, reaching the Siegfried Line on 31 January. This vaunted defensive barrier did not slow them and they pushed on into Germany. On 6 February, they were relieved and moved to the Huertgen Forest area where they continued to advance on the Roer River until 17 February when they were pulled back to their base near Rheims.

On 26 December the 3rd Army had delivered the "Screaming Eagles" Christmas present one day late as they lifted the siege of Bastogne, although German pressure continued for the next few days. Finally, on 13 January, the 101st went over to the attack taking their primary objective, Bourcy, by the 17th. On 26 January, the tough airborne troops were assigned to the 7th Army in Alsace to defend positions along the German border until late February when the 101st was also pulled back to positions near Rheims.

The 17th Airborne Division had also received its "blooding" in the Battle of the Bulge. Bad flying weather had delayed the "Talons from Heaven" from being deployed to the continent until Christmas Eve when they were immediately sent into defensive positions along the Meuse River. Then on 3 January, the 17th was assigned to the 3rd Army where they were used to take towns west of Bastogne to prevent the Germans from attacking that crossroads from the rear. During these operations, SGT Isadore Jachman of the 513th PIR won a Congressional Medal of Honor for knocking out German tanks with a bazooka.

After securing the area west of Bastogne, the 17th Airborne struck east across Luxembourg, crossed the Roer River into Germany and drove towards the Siegfried Line. Finally on 10 February, the 17th was relieved and moved back to Chalons-sur-Marne, France.

Although the Battle of the Bulge had proven costly for the Allies and had thrown a scare into Eisenhower, it was far more costly for the Germans. The American troops, heartened by the heroic 101st Airborne stand at Bastogne, had rallied and driven the Germans back to the borders of Germany. In the process of this last fight, Hitler had expended any remaining strategic reserves he had, losing 220,000 troops and 1,400 tanks in the process.

In the aftermath of the Bulge fighting, some reorganization took place among the airborne troops. The heroic 509th Parachute Infantry Battalion, now down to seven officers and 48 men, was disbanded and the troops assigned to the 82nd Airborne. The 551st Parachute Infantry Battalion was now down to about 100 officers and men, and was also deactivated and its troops assigned to the 82nd. To give it some combat experienced troops, the newly arrived 13th Airborne Division, which had reached France in late January, had the 517th Parachute Combat Team assigned. Also deactivated in late February was the 17th Airborne's 193rd Glider Infantry regiment and attached 550th Glider Infantry Battalion, the latter forming the basis for a third battalion of the 194th Glider Infantry.

With four U.S. airborne divisions now in the theater, one operation which was considered was a coup de main airborne assault on Berlin by the British 6th, U.S. 17th, and U.S. 82nd Airborne divisions. Since it had been decided to let the Russians take Berlin, this operation never got past the planning stages.

A paratrooper of the 17th Airborne Division serving with Patton's Third Army examines a captured German machine gun in a small town in Luxembourg during January of 1945. (U.S. Army)

Two troopers of the 82nd Airborne Division take a break in the snow and read reports of their fighting during the Battle of the Bulge in the GI newspaper "STARS AND STRIPES." (U.S. Army)

Operation VARSITY: The Last Big Jump In Europe

With the drive on Germany now reaching its climax, 24 March 1945 was set as the date for crossing the Rhine in force near Wesel. LTGEN Sir Miles Dempsey was selected to command the forces carrying out the crossing. The Corps HQ, U.S. 17th Airborne, and British 6th Airborne were assigned from the XVIIIth Airborne Corps. Initially, the U.S. 13th Airborne was also assigned, but the lack of transport aircraft led them to be scratched from the operation. The mission for the airborne troops was a highly important one; they were to take the *Diersfordter* forest, which occupied heights that would allow German artillery to interdict the crossing. In addition to knocking out any German artillery on the heights, the airborne troops were also to seize bridges across the Issel River to assist the Allied breakout once the Rhine barrier was breached.

Unlike previous operations in which the airborne assault had preceded other portions of the operation, it was decided that in VARSITY, as the airborne phase of the crossing was code named, the airborne troops would not be inserted until the other assault troops had crossed the Rhine. This would allow intensive artillery preparation against the *Diersfordter* forest and would allow the airborne troops to come in during daylight.

The 6th Airborne had the mission of jumping into the northern portions of the airhead, while the 17th Airborne would come into the southern portion. The airhead itself was actually rather compact for two divisions, with four paratroop DZs and six glider LZs. All airborne troops would come in on D-Day. Making their task somewhat easier was the fact that all of the DZs and LZs were within range of Allied artillery support from across the Rhine.

At 0100 on 24 March, over 2,000 artillery pieces opened a barrage against the German positions east of the Rhine, To ground German air power and stall reinforcements, 1,500 Allied bombers hit German airfields and reserve concentrations. With this massive support, Allied infantry and combat engineers carried out their assault crossing against light opposition.

Then just before 1000, 1,696 troop transports (mostly C-46s), 1,346 gliders and 2,153 fighter aircraft arrived over the DZs. Although twenty-two aircraft were shot down, the fact that the C-46 Commando had two exit doors allowed all of the paratroopers to clear the Commandos before they crashed.

First out the doors over the DZs for the 17th Airborne were the men of Edson Raff's 507th Parachute Infantry. A substantial portion of the 507th, including Raff, was dropped two miles northwest of their DZ, while the remainder of the regiment and the 464th Parachute Field Artillery were dropped right on target. Raff quickly gathered those paratroopers who had landed off course and rejoined the rest of his men in time to knock out a battery of German artillery firing on the assault troops crossing the Rhine. By 1400 on D-Day, the 507th had secured all of its objectives and had given the new 57MM and 75MM recoilless rifles their successful baptism of fire against German tanks. Much more effective than the bazooka, the recoilless rifles gave the American paratroopers far more tank-killing capability than any previous operation.

As with other airborne generals throughout the war, the 17th's commander, MGEN Miley, found himself in combat soon after landing as he manned a machine gun, along with a couple of other paratroopers.

The 513th PIR dropped after the 507th and was also off course, landing near Hamminkeln in the British sector. As it turned out, Hamminkeln contained heavily fortified

LTCOL T.B. Johnson of the 139th Airborne Engineers briefs his troops on their upcoming mission with the aid of wall charts and aerial photographs before departing for Operation VARSITY. (U.S. Army)

German artillery batteries so the American paratroopers immediately began attacking. They were soon supported by the British glider troops who had been scheduled to land near Hamminkeln. Thus reinforced, they succeeded in knocking out the artillery and taking the town of Hamminkeln, freeing up the glider troops to seize the bridges across the Issel. During this operation, PFC Stuart Stryker of the 513th won a posthumous Congressional Medal of Honor. As with the 507th PIR, by 1400 the 513th had secured all of its objectives, taking 1,152 German prisoners in the process.

The 194th Glider Infantry had the mission of protecting the airhead's right flank and seizing a crossing over the Issel. The two tow aircraft delivered the glider riders right onto their LZs, but these proved to be in the midst of a large concentration of German artillery. On landing, the glider troops had to go immediately into action. So effective was the assault by the 194th that they knocked out forty-two artillery pieces, ten tanks, two flak wagons and five self-propelled guns as well as taking about 1,000 prisoners.

The British were equally successful with their objectives as the 3rd and 5th Parachute Brigades cleared their areas, the latter helping with the attack on Hamminkeln as well. The 6th Air Landing Brigade was also successful in taking all of its objectives. By 1400, all American and British airborne objectives had been secured. Although the day had gone well for the American paratroopers and glider troops, the 17th Airborne Division had still suffered 1,521 casualties.

During the operation, LTGEN Ridgway got another chance to put his trusty Springfield rifle to use when, while returning from the 6th Airborne Command Post (CP) early in the morning of D+1, he got in a firefight with a German patrol.

Back in his own HQ with the British 6th Guards armored Brigade attached to his XVIIIth Airborne Corps, Ridgway was in command of the attack eastward into Germany on 26 March. As they advanced on 27 March, the 194th Glider Infantry ran into heavy resistance just outside Lembeck. As they punched through the German defenders, SGT Clinton M. Hendrick won a Congressional Medal of Honor for killing all of the German defenders of one castle. Riding atop tanks, in commandeered vehicles, or even on horseback, the airborne troops continued to push into Germany. By 28 March, the XVIIIth Airborne Corps had already taken 7,000 prisoners.

As Patton's Third Army drove up from the south to link up with the troops advancing after the Rhine crossing, over 350,000 Germans were sealed into a pocket in the Ruhr industrial area. While reducing this pocket, the 17th Airborne Division was assigned to take the important industrial city of Essen. The 507th PIR fought their way into the city on 10 April, capturing industrialist Alfred Krupp in the process. During the reduction of the Ruhr Pocket, the 13th Airborne Division remained in reserve, while the 101st held defensive positions along the Rhine opposite Dusseldorf to help seal the Germans in the pocket. The 82nd Airborne crossed the Rhine and seized the city of Cologne.

Members of the 17th Airborne Division wait to board their gliders during Operation VARSITY. These troopers are armed with M1 Carbines, a Bazooka, a .30 caliber air-cooled machine gun, and M1 Garand rifles. (U.S. Army)

Troopers of the 17th airborne help each other check their equipment before Operation VARSITY. The men are equipped with life jackets because their jump involved a large river – the Rhine. The paratrooper on the right has his M1 Carbine secured in a case/holster. (IWM)

Carbines

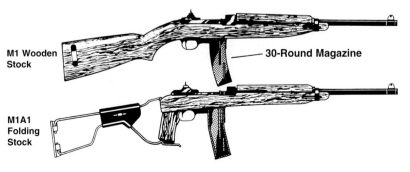

M1 Wooden Stock

M1A1 Folding Stock

30-Round Magazine

35

After finishing the reduction of this pocket, the XVIIIth Airborne Corps, now comprised of the U.S. 82nd Airborne, British 6th Airborne U.S. 7th Armored Division and U.S. 8th Infantry Division, was ordered to attack northward to cut off the Danish peninsula isolating those German troops remaining there. On 30 April, the airborne troops linked up with the Russians at the Elbe, then on 2 May, Berlin fell. There were still serious fears among Allied commanders, however, that the Germans would stage a final defiant stand in their "Alpine Fortress," and as a result, on the same day that Berlin fell to the Russians, the 101st Airborne Division along with other U.S. and French units struck towards Hitler's Alpine retreat at Berchtesgaden.

This final drive proved anti-climactic as the Germans surrendered on 7 May. Still, the 101st captured a train loaded with priceless art treasures on a siding outside of Berchtesgaden. Specially trained members of the division, many of them art historians or members of museum staffs in civilian life, immediately took charge of the looted artwork.

XVIIIth Airborne Corps soon received notification that the 13th and 101st Airborne Division should prepare for redeployment to the Pacific, though the 101st continued to occupy parts of Southern Germany and Austria for the time being. The 82nd Airborne Division moved to Berlin to occupy the American sector, while the 508th PIR was detached to occupy Frankfurt. The dropping of the Atomic bombs on Japan on 6 and 9 August led to the Japanese surrender on 14 August, thus eliminating the need to redeploy the two airborne divisions to the Pacific.

A C-47 and a Waco CG-4 glider take off for Operation VARSITY while others form up overhead. The combination of C-47s and CG-4s were used in every airborne operation undertaken by U.S. troops in Europe. (U.S. Army)

Members of the 466th Parachute Field Artillery HQ Battery check their parachutes before enplaning during Operation VARSITY. The trooper in the foreground carries his .45 Colt M1911 semi-automatic pistol in a shoulder holster. (U.S. Army)

A 17th Airborne Division Horsa glider lies in a field in Germany with its rear end detached. The lightweight ramps are in place and its load, probably a Jeep, has departed. British Horsa gliders were used to transport larger items of equipment that would not fit into a CG-4. (U.S. Army)

Glider troops taking part in Operation VARSITY move out toward their objective after landing. The trooper in the foreground is armed with an M1A1 folding stock Carbine. (U.S. Army)

This trooper of the 507th Parachute Infantry, 17th Airborne Division, dangles in his harness after his parachute became caught in a tree during the jump across the Rhine. (U.S. Army)

Paratroop Switchblade Knife

37

Members of the 17th Airborne Division form into units after their jump across the Rhine in March of 1945. Operation VARSITY was the last large scale paratroop operation in Europe. (U.S. Army)

Members of the 513th Parachute Infantry wait for British tanks to move ahead before entering Munster, Germany. The trooper in the left foreground is armed with an M1A1 folding stock Carbine. (U.S. Army)

Members of the 513th Parachute Infantry take cover during their advance after the Operation VARSITY landings. They have been joined by a British paratrooper armed with an Owen sub-machine gun. (U.S. Army)

57MM Recoilless Rifle

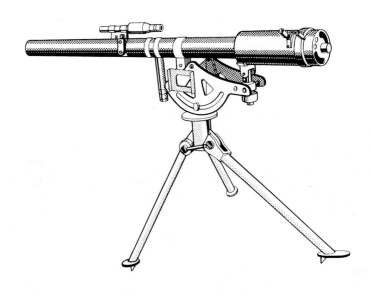

As they pass a British tank on the road into Munster during Operation VARSITY, 17th Airborne troops pick up additional .30 caliber M1 Garand ammunition clips pre-packaged in bandoleers. The trooper in the foreground has at least three bandoleers. (U.S. Army)

17th Airborne paratroopers advance past bombed out buildings into the outskirts of Munster, Germany after their successful jump across the Rhine during Operation VARSITY. (U.S. Army)

A trooper of the 505th Parachute Infantry raised the American flag over a German castle which the 505th requisitioned as their Headquarters during April of 1945. (U.S. Army)

Members of the 505th Parachute Infantry relax in the German castle that was taken over as their headquarters/billet during April of 1945. (U.S. Army)

A member of the 82nd Airborne Division patrols outside the fence line at Wobbelin Concentration Camp which was liberated by the "All Americans" late in the war. (U.S. Army)

Paratroopers of the 82nd Airborne prepare to board boxcars at Duren for transport into Northern Germany during late April of 1945. The trucks are GMC two and a half ton 4 X 6 cargo trucks. (U.S. Army)

MGEN Maxwell Taylor, Commander of the 101st Airborne Division, accepts the official surrender of remaining German SS troops in the Schwendt area of Austria on 9 May 1945. (U.S. Army)

Airborne Against Japan: Nadzab Airfield

The first Army airborne unit deployed to the Pacific Theater was the 503rd Parachute Infantry which was assigned directly to MacArthur's HQ. The 503rd had been in Australia since December of 1942, but it was not until the summer of 1943 that they would make their first operational jump. During GEN MacArthur's battle for New Guinea, the seizure of the city of Lae was of primary importance prior to moving into the Huon Peninsula. Rather than strike directly at Lae and face a staunch Japanese defense, MacArthur first ordered a feint towards Salamaua to weaken the Lae defenses. The 9th Australian Infantry Division was scheduled to make an amphibious landing east of Lae; then, on D+1, the 503rd PIR would be dropped to seize an airstrip at the town of Nadzab west of Lae. Australian engineers who had infiltrated through the jungle would meet the paratroopers after they had secured the airstrip and prepared it so that the 7th Australian Division could be air landed to strike at Lae from the west.

In preparation for this mission, the 503rd was deployed to Port Moresby on 18 August 1943 and ordered to prepare for a jump on Nadzab on 5 September. Battalion missions were broken down as follows; the 1/503 would jump directly onto the airstrip and clear it of any Japanese defenders, the 2/503 would jump and secure the village of Gabsonkek to the west and secure the 1/503's flank, and the 3/503 would jump and secure the village of Gabmatzung to the east. To give the paratrooper's artillery support in case of counterattack,

two Australian 25-pounder guns and their crews would be dropped an hour after the jump by the 503rd.

To maintain secrecy, the 503rd paratroopers did not receive this mission briefing until 4 September. The Australian 9th Infantry Division had already landed 20 miles east of Lae against light opposition, although they had been attacked by Japanese aircraft. On the morning of 5 September, fog and rain initially made it appear as if the jump might have to be aborted; however, conditions improved and before 0900 the 503rd was in the air. A few minutes before 1030 after preliminary airstrikes, the 503rd began jumping.

The drop was unopposed, but there were still three deaths and thirty-three injuries, two of the deaths attributable to faulty parachutes which did not open. Once on the ground, assembly proved difficult due to the 10 to 12-foot high Kunai grass. The high grass also caused some paratrooper's to start firing at each other, believing they had encountered the enemy, but fortunately only two paratroopers were slightly wounded. The Aussie artillery was dropped and was quickly assembled and prepared for action by its crews. With the airstrip secured, the engineers began clearing it, aided by two bulldozers and twelve flame throwers, which had been flown in.

The engineers worked through the night, while the paratroopers provided security, and at about 1200 on D+1 the Australian 7th Infantry Division began air landing and immediately moving out towards Lae, which fell to the combined Australian attack on 16 September. Some Japanese retreating from the battle around Lae ran into paratroopers from the 503rd, which resulted in some firefights, but with their mission successfully completed, the 503rd was pulled back to Port Moresby on 17 September.

Paratroops of the 503rd Parachute Infantry land on Kamiri airstrip, Noemfoor Island on 2 July 1944. The troops were landing on a secure airfield captured earlier by the 158th Regimental Combat Team (RCT). (U.S. Army)

The 503rd Parachute Infantry was dropped onto Kamiri airstrip after the commander of the 158th RCT was told there were roughly twice the number of Japanese on the island as had been originally estimated. (U.S. Army)

41

Noemfoor Island

The 11th Airborne Division had its own jump school since MGEN Swing, the division commander, wanted each trooper in the division to be both glider and parachute qualified. As a result, when the 11th sailed for the Pacific in May of 1944, it was the most versatile of the five U.S. airborne divisions. While the 11th was bound for New Guinea, MacArthur's troops had continued their advance along the coast of that large island to seize airstrips to support further operations. Then on 27 May, American troops landed on Biak where they met heavy resistance. The Japanese were sending in reinforcements from Noemfoor Island and, as a result, MacArthur ordered Noemfoor taken. In addition to knocking out this source of Japanese reinforcements, MacArthur also wanted the two complete and one partially completed airfields on the island.

Initial intelligence estimates were that 3,250 Japanese were defending Noemfoor. To defeat this force, LTGEN Walter Krueger, who MacArthur had put in charge of planning the attack, had the Army's 158th Regimental Combat Team (RCT) plus some aviation engineer battalions. In reserve were the 34th Infantry Regiment and the 503rd Parachute Infantry Regiment which had been carrying out patrols on New Guinea to eliminate Japanese stragglers around Hollandia.

The softening up of Noemfoor began on 20 June and continued until just before the assault at 0800 on 2 July. With little opposition, the assault troops secured the beachhead, one airstrip and high ground overlooking the beachhead almost immediately. They then, however, began to face stiffening Japanese resistance. From a prisoner, they learned that 3,000 additional Japanese troops had arrived as reinforcements, meaning that the 158th RCT was facing twice the number of defenders as originally thought. As a result, a request was sent at 1115 for the 503rd PIR to be dropped as reinforcements.

Since Kamiri Air Field was already in U.S. hands, it was decided to drop one parachute infantry battalion each day over the next three days as reinforcements. At 1000 on 3 July the 1/503rd began jumping; however, the presence of many amphibious assault vehicles parked on the air strip caused almost ten percent of the 739 paratroopers jumping to be injured. For the 3/503rd's jump the next day a number of precautions were taken and the vehicles were pulled off of the air strip, but injuries still ran to 8% of the jumpers. As a result of this high jump injury rate, it was decided to bring the 2/503rd in over the beach on the 5th.

As it turned out, however, none of the jump injuries were necessary as the report of additional Japanese troops proved to be false. In fact, there were only 2,500 defenders on the island. Still, since the paratroopers were there, they were given the toughest assignment: to mop up the Japanese left on the southern part of the island, which contained peaks and jungle. For the next month, the men of the 503rd fought against tenacious Japanese defenders who would fade away just before the paratroopers could finish them off. During one of these actions, SGT Ray Eubanks of the 2/503rd won a posthumous Congressional Medal of Honor for single-handedly knocking out a Japanese machine gun position. The mopping up operations continued into August, with the last of the Japanese finally being eliminated on 17 August. During more than six weeks of combat on the island, the 503rd killed about 1,000 enemy soldiers. On 28 August, the 503rd was moved back to Kamiri Air Strip where they became the 503rd PCT a few days later with the addition of the 462nd Parachute Field Artillery Battalion and the 161st Parachute Engineer Battalion. The 503rd remained on Noemfoor until November when the unit moved to Leyte and went into reserve.

A member of the 503rd Parachute Infantry gathers his parachute after the jump on Noemfoor Island. He is armed with an M1 Thompson SMG and carriers magazine pouches on his pistol belt which hold five spare twenty round magazines each. (U.S. Army)

The Philippines – Leyte

On 20 October 1944, MacArthur finally kept his promise to return to the Philippines by landing four division on the island of Leyte. As it fought its way inland, the Sixth Army under LTGEN Walter Krueger began to run into trouble. As a result, the 11th Airborne Division, which had been undergoing jungle training on New Guinea, arrived on 18 November as reinforcements. Four days later, the airborne troops were attached to the XXIV Corps. Initially, the 187th Glider Infantry was assigned to guard the Corps' rear areas, while the 188th Glider infantry was assigned the mission of securing the area between Bugho and La Paz. Offensive operations against the Japanese positions fell primarily upon the 511th PIR.

The 511th began its attack on 28 November through the Mahonag Mountains towards Ormoc Bay. The combination of difficult terrain and resistance slowed their progress. The paratroopers also felt the lack of artillery support as they attempted to assault the Japanese position and A Battery, 457th Parachute Field Artillery (PFA) was dropped in to give support with their 75MM Pack Howitzers. Early in December, the Japanese counterattacked toward the airfields held by the Americans. This attack was spearheaded by a jump of 300 Japanese paratroopers on the night of 6 December against the San Pablo airstrip. The 11th Airborne CP being located near the airstrip, MGEN Swing, the 11th commander, actually witnessed the Japanese drop. Quickly drawing on his 127th Parachute Engineer Battalion and the 674th Parachute Field Artillery Battalion, Swing organized an immediate counterattack.

By daybreak, Swing's hastily assembled force had retaken the airstrip and turned mopping up operations over to the 187th GIR. Even while this Japanese effort was being nipped in the bud, the 511th had started attacking again on 7 December, the third anniversary of the Pearl Harbor attack. Reinforced by a battalion of the 187th Glider Infantry, the 511th gained ground, although the paratroopers and glidermen had to fight off Japanese "Banzai" attacks.

During one such attack, PFC Elmer Fryer won a posthumous Congressional Medal of Honor for single-handedly killing 27 Japanese attempting to outflank his company. On 17 December, the 511th finally fought through to the coast and set up defensive positions where they remained until Christmas Day when they were relieved and sent back to the divisional base camp. The 1/187th and 1/188th finished mopping up Japanese resistance at Anonang in two days of heavy combat, killing some 238 Japanese before finally securing their objectives. By mid-January of 1945, the entire 11th Airborne had been pulled back to its base camp to prepare for its next mission.

Liberation of Manila

On 9 January 1945, U.S. troops landed on the island of Luzon. In support of the advance on Manila, the 11th Airborne was assigned the mission of carrying out a combined amphibious/parachute assault to seize Tagaytay Ridge south of Manila. This was key high ground overlooking the road to the capital. The 11th's mission was in support of a second landing by two American divisions on 29 January. 31 January was selected as the date for the amphibious landing by the 187th and 188th Glider Infantry Regiments at Nasugbu. Once ashore they were to drive to Route 17. The other portion of the operation would be carried out by the 511th PIR and the 457 PFA who would jump onto Tagaytay Ridge and hold it until the glider troops reached them. Opposing the 11th would be about 7,000 Japanese troops defending the Nasugbu and Tagaytay area, mostly between Tagaytay Ridge and Route 17.

About 0830 on 31 January, the 188th GIR began coming ashore followed by the 187th and, leaving the 1/187th to guard the beachhead, had reached Route 17 by noon and already moved on towards Tagaytay Ridge. On the morning of 1 February they finally ran into heavy opposition from the Japanese who were well dug in on two peaks that rose to over 2,000 feet.

The 511th and 457th were initially supposed to jump in on 2 February but the drop was postponed until 3 February while the battle between the Ridge and Route 17 raged. A shortage of C-47s meant that the paratroopers would have to make three separate drops. To avoid misdrops, pathfinders had infiltrated through the jungle and set up beacons on top of Tagaytay Ridge. Nevertheless, only about one-third of the 915 paratroopers in the first wave dropped on target. About 540 jumped five miles short of the DZ, and had to march to the ridge, reaching it on the afternoon of 3 February. Unfortunately, the second group of paratroopers saw the discarded parachutes of those who had jumped short and jumped short as well. By 1500, however, the paratroopers and glider troops had linked up along Route 17. The last of the paratroopers jumped in on the morning of 4 February.

Using captured or borrowed trucks, the airborne troops reached the Paranaque River about four miles from Naila where they hit the Japanese Genko Line, which included well-sited concrete pillboxes. The 11th was assigned to drive through the Genko Line and on into Manila. On the morning of 5 February the attack began with the 511th first through the line, followed closely by the two glider infantry regiments. Over the next week the men of the 11th clawed their way through the line, running into especially heavy

Non-parachute qualified replacement troops for the 11th Airborne Division undergo parachute harness training on Luzon, Philippine Islands during May of 1945. The 11th Airborne had its own jump school and all troopers in the 11th were both glider and parachute qualified. (U.S. Army)

fighting at Nichols Field and Fort McKinley. In many instances, the Japanese defenders had to be cleared house-to-house and bunker-to-bunker. During the heavy battle for Fort McKinley, PFC Manuel Perez, Jr. of the 511th PIR won a Congressional Medal of Honor. Manila was finally liberated on 21 February, although the 1st Cavalry Division beat the airborne troopers into the city. During the drive from the beaches to the capital, the 11th Airborne Division had suffered about 900 casualties but had killed some 3,000 Japanese.

Jumping Onto the Rock

The fall of the island fortress of Corregidor had marked one of the low points of the war against Japan. As a result, when "The Rock," now occupied by the Japanese, proved to be a thorn in MacArthur's side, he ordered it to be retaken both for its symbolic value and because it controlled access to Manila Bay. The plan for retaking "The Rock" called for a combined airborne/amphibious assault. The parachute portion was to be under-taken by the 503rd RCT, MacArthur's favorite airborne unit, while the amphibious landings were to be carried out by the 3/34th Infantry Regiment. Corregidor was quite heavily defended by about 5,000 Japanese troops, mostly tough Naval Landing Troops (Marines). Expecting an amphibious assault, the defenders were well dug in facing the beaches.

The plan evolved by COL George Jones, commander of the 503rd PCT, and his staff called for one-third of the parachute assault force (compromised primarily of the 3/

503rd PIR, Company C, 161st Airborne Engineers and Battery I, 462nd PFA) to drop on the high ground, known as "Topside." The site of a former barracks, "Topside" offered a parade ground and golf course, which could be used as DZs. One of this force's missions would be to secure the DZ for a second wave, which would jump that afternoon. This force would include the 2/503rd, the service company, Battery B/462nd PF, and the remainder of the HQ Company. Together this force would clear "Topside" of any Japanese. Finally, on D+1, the 1/503rd and Battery A/462nd PFA would jump in to be deployed as needed to clear the island.

Dropping troops on a small island was the biggest difficulty faced by the paratroopers and their transport crews. As a result, it was decided to approach at only 500 feet, with only six paratroopers able to jump on each pass from each C-47. Estimates of jump casualties ran as high as 50%.

Air Corps and Naval preparatory bombardment was especially heavy just prior to the assault to drive the Japanese under cover as the drop planes came over. This barrage ended just minutes before the paratroopers began to jump. Despite the heavy bombardment, few Japanese were killed by it, being too well dug in, Nevertheless, there are indications the bombardment did sever many of the Japanese field telephone lines, thus limiting their ability to communicate with each other.

The first few sticks out of their aircraft drifted too far south so Jones quickly adjusted the approach path and release point of the transports. The Japanese, although extremely well prepared for an amphibious assault, were caught completely by surprise as the paratroopers descended overhead. Adding to the confusion was the fact that the commander of the island's defense, Imperial Japanese Navy CAPT Itogaki, and his staff were killed in the first few minutes of the assault by a paratrooper's grenade.

Although the dreaded 50% casualty figure was avoided, there were 25% casualties on the drop and in the fighting immediately after the drop. Many, however, were jump injuries, which did not prevent the tough paratroopers from fighting. Shortly after the paratroopers had jumped into combat on "Topside", the infantrymen landed on "Black Beach" unopposed since the paratroopers were occupying the defender's attention.

Paratroopers of the 511th Parachute Infantry, 11th Airborne Division, reassemble after a drop on Luzon during January of 1945. The jeep is configured as a communication vehicle with radios and its own generator in the towed trailer. (U.S. Army)

Paratroopers of the 511th Parachute Infantry 'chute up for the drop on Tagaytay Ridge, Luzon, Philippines during January of 1945. The trooper in the right foreground is armed with an M1A1 Carbine. (U.S. Army)

Once ashore, the leg infantry took Malinta Hill with only slight casualties.

At 1240, the next group of paratroopers began jumping, putting 2,050 members of the 503rd PCT on the ground when they completed their descents. Their casualties were somewhat less, at 15%, which included some paratroopers killed by Japanese snipers during their descent and fourteen others who died from landing injuries amidst the rubble of the former buildings on "Topside."

Supported by their parachute artillerymen, the parachute infantrymen spent the rest of D-Day clearing "Topside". Once they had it secured, the jump the next day proved to be unnecessary so, to avoid more jumping injuries, COL Jones ordered the rest of his men to come in over the beach on the afternoon of 17 February. The Japanese began coming out of their holes on the night of 17/18 February, but they struck mostly at the positions of the 34th Infantry.

The paratroopers turn came at 0600 on 19 February when Japanese marines poured out onto "Topside." By the time the hand-to-hand combat had ended, there were 500 dead Japanese at a cost of thirty-three paratroopers killed and seventy-five wounded. PVT Lloyd McCarter won the Congressional Medal of Honor during this battle. The next two days were spent mopping up any Japanese marines who had survived the slaughter.

There still remained approximately 2,000 Japanese trapped in a tunnel under Malinta Hill. Their plan apparently was to blow open an exit and then launch a massive suicide charge. The plan literally backfired when most of them were killed in the explosion. Most of the survivors then retreated to the "tail" of the tadpole-shaped island. On 24 February, Jones's paratroopers began clearing this area. Most of their casualties came when the Japanese blew up another tunnel, killing and injuring 200 paratroopers. By 27 February, the island had been secured. In the process, the Americans had killed 4,500 Japanese and taken only twenty prisoners. The remainder of the defenders were presumed buried beneath the island's rocky surface. 455 Americans had died and 550 others had become casualties while retaking "The Rock."

During the second week in March, the 503rd RCT was transported to Mindoro. In addition to adopting a new insignia commemorating the jump on Corregidor, the 503rd was scheduled for another jump on the island of Negros. Instead, the paratroopers were landed by boat on 3 April and attached to the 40th Division to help clear the remaining Japanese defenders from the island. They were still on Negros at the end of the war.

Discarded parachutes littering the landscape near Topside Barracks on the island of Corregidor show the pattern of the drop by members of the 503rd during their airborne assault on the island. (U.S. Army)

Two paratroopers of the 503rd Parachute Infantry take cover amidst smoke from gasoline being used to burn the Japanese defenders of Corregidor out of their tunnels. Both troopers have grenade launchers attached to their M1 Garand rifles. (U.S. Army)

Members of the 3rd Battalion, 503rd Parachute Infantry jump from Douglas C-47s of the 54th Troop Carrier Wing over the island of Corregidor in Manila Bay. The retaking of Corregidor was both politically and militarily important. (U.S. Army)

Airborne artillerymen of D Battery, 462nd Parachute Artillery, 11th Airborne Division assemble their 75MM Pack Howitzers under fire after dropping on Corregidor Island. (U.S. Army)

Members of the 503rd Parachute Infantry advance across Corregidor. The island had been devastated by the pre-invasion naval bombardment and heavy bombing by both Navy and USAAF aircraft. A destroyer lies offshore to lend fire support if called upon. (U.S. Army)

General of the Army Douglas MacArthur, along with paratroopers of the 503rd Parachute Infantry, salutes the Stars and Stripes as it was raised once again over Corregidor – "The Rock." (U.S. Army)

Rescue at Los Banos

On 4 February 1945, MGEN Swing was ordered, in secret, to prepare a plan to liberate 2,200 civilians from a prison camp at Los Banos. Located on a large lake named *Laguna de Bay*, the camp was deep in Japanese controlled territory. The 11th Airborne, at the time Swing received his orders, was still fighting along the Genko Line, but he ordered his intelligence staff to gather as much information as possible about the camp. Among their sources of information was an escapee who, being an engineer, was able to draw a very detailed map of the camp.

The plan called for the division recon platoon and some Philippine guerrillas to infiltrate near the camp by boat. Their mission would be to secure a stretch of shoreline, get in position to attack the camp's guard towers and strongpoints, and secure a DZ next to the camp. Two minutes before the parachute drop on the DZ, the recon platoon would ignite White phosphorus grenades to guide in a paratroop company. Simultaneously, the recon platoon would hit the guard positions then, joined by the paratroopers, advance into the camp to liberate the prisoners.

Three more parachute companies would come over the beach in amphibious tractors (Amtracs). The paratroopers would then secure the beachhead while the Amtracs proceeded to the camp to pick up the freed prisoners. To remove some of the potential danger, a battalion of glider infantry would launch a diversionary attack to tie down possible Japanese reinforcements.

0700 on 23 February was set as H-Hour, Company A, 1/511th PIR would carry out the jump, while the rest of the 511th plus Battery D, 457th PFA would come in via the Amtracs. If the 1/511th and the artillerymen had to fight their way clear after the prisoners were evacuated, they would strike north along the shore of *Laguna de Bay* towards the glider infantrymen of the 1/188th who were carrying out the diversionary attack.

About 0200 on 22 February, the recon platoon and the guerrillas landed near the camp and went into hiding in the jungle until the next night. On the morning of 23 February, the 1/188th launched their diversionary attack. Smoke grenades were emplaced by 0658 on the 23rd, and the paratroopers began their descent a couple of minutes later, just as the recon platoon hit the guard positions as hard as they could. As soon as they had landed and divested themselves of their parachutes, the paratroopers joined in the attack on the camp. Within twenty minutes the camp was secure, with all 243 Japanese guards being killed in the process. Amazingly, no prisoners or troops were injured during the attack. The prisoners were successfully evacuated in the Amtracs, which later made a return trip to pick up the few remaining prisoners, the paratroopers and the guerrillas. By about 1200 on the 23rd, the 1/188th had broken off their diversionary attack as well.

In the wake of their incredible success at Los Banos, the 11th Airborne was assigned on 6 March to mop up Japanese resistance on southern Luzon, an operation that continued until late April.

First Into Japan

After the Japanese had been mopped up in southern Luzon and resistance had ceased on 1 May 1945, the 11th Airborne Division established a new base camp at Lipa Airstrip. Heavy fighting continued elsewhere on Luzon to prevent the Japanese still resisting from being evacuated, "Gypsy Task Force," drawn from the 11th's 1/511th, Companies G & I of the 511th, Battery C, 457th PFA, and Company C, 127th Airborne Engineers, as well as miscellaneous other personnel, was formed to parachute and glider land at Camalaniugan Airstrip. There, they would march to Appari on the coast to prevent the Japanese from using it as an evacuation port. Even through U.S. ground troops reached the objective before the drop at 0900 on 23 June, the landing went ahead to get as many troops as possible in position to oppose a possible Japanese attempt at withdrawal.

Soon after this operation had ended, the 541st PIR arrived from the States to join the 11th, but rather than joining as a regiment, the unit was broken up as replacements. At 0530 on 11 August, the 11th Airborne was alerted for movement to Okinawa as a stopping off point for the occupation of Japan. Once on Okinawa, the "Angels," the nickname gained by the 11th from missionaries they had liberated at Los Banos, waited around until 30 August when the first troops took off to occupy Japan. First off the aircraft at Atsugi Airfield outside Tokyo was MGEN Swing. The 11th Airborne would remain in Japan for the next four years, serving on occupation duty until 1949.

Paratroops of the 11th Airborne exit a Curtiss C-46 Commando. The Commando had exit doors on both sides of the fuselage allowing the paratroopers to exit more quickly and be less spread out than with the Douglas C-47. (U.S. Army)

C-47s of "Gypsy Task Force" enroute to Appari on the Luzon coast. Although U.S. ground units had already arrived in Appari, it was decided to proceed with the drop in order to reinforce the blocking forces already in place. (U.S. Army)

Members of the 11th Airborne prepare to receive a supply drop from a USAAF L-5 spotter aircraft. The 11th used Lipa airfield as a base camp for "mopping up" operations in Luzon. The 11th stayed in the Philippines until 11 August 1945. (U.S. Army)

The 11th Airborne was used to block any attempt by the Japanese to withdraw their troops from the Philippines. On 23 June 1945, "Gypsy Task Force" jumped on Appari on the Luzon coast to block the fleeing Japanese. (U.S. Army)

11th Airborne paratroopers stand guard at the Grant Hotel in Yokohama. The first member of the 11th Airborne to set foot in Japan was MGEN Swing, who arrived on 30 August 1945. (U.S. Army)

A pair of 11th Airborne paratroopers stand guard duty in Yokohama, Japan after the Japanese surrender. The 11th remained in Japan on occupation duty until 1949. (U.S. Army)

The War Is Over

Of the five airborne divisions formed during the Second World War, only two would remain on active duty in the early post war years. Because of its occupation duties, the 11th Airborne Division continued to serve in the Pacific, returning to Fort Campbell, KY in May of 1949. The 17th Airborne Division was deactivated in September of 1945, to be followed by the 101st Airborne in November of the same year. Initially it appeared that the 101st would remain on duty at Fort Bragg, while the 82nd Airborne would be disbanded; however, members of the 82nd lobbied hard for their continued existence and the fact that the 82nd had seen more combat than the 101st led to the decision in November of 1945 to retain the 82nd and disband the 101st.

The "Screaming Eagles" came back into existence a couple of times during the post-war years, finally becoming a regular airborne unit again during 1956 and serving today as the U.S. Air Assault Division. The 13th Airborne Division was deactivated in February of 1946 and the 11th Airborne ended up in Germany during the Cold War, being deactivated in 1958. Although reactivated in 1963 as the Test Air Assault Division, the 11th was again deactivated in 1965 when the 1st Cav became the air assault division.